"*While we know much more about litera
ago, we continue to miss the mark on the i
are failing millions of kids and widening th
text, Shawn Robinson and Corey Thompso
to change how we perceive, diagnose, and teach African American children
with dyslexia. More importantly, they insist that we rethink our approach
to and investment in research related to the intersectionality of reading,
disability, and race. Both teachers and researchers should take note!*"

Timothy Dohrer is Director of the Master of Science in
Education Program, Northwestern University, USA

"*Dr. Shawn Robinson has compiled an impressive collection of work by
distinguished researchers on the subject of African American boys with
dyslexia. This perennially underserved population in far too many ways.
Our institutional failure to ensure early identification and appropriate
instruction diminishes opportunities for individuals to reach their full
potential to often tragic results. This volume is a welcome addition to the
scarce resources on the subject, and offers the hope that its lessons will
improve individual lives, as well as the health of our communities.*"

Cheri Rae is Author of *DyslexiaLand: A Guide for
Parents of Children with Dyslexia* and Director of The
Dyslexia Project, Santa Barbara, USA

"*This highly readable book addresses two of the most pressing issues in
education – the inequities of achievement gaps and the importance of early
reading as the gateway to education. The authors are authoritative experts
who share important ideas, findings, and practical steps that can be taken
to help all children learn to read.*"

John D.E. Gabrieli is Grover Hermann Professor of Health Sciences
and Technology and Cognitive Neuroscience at Harvard-MIT
Division of Health Sciences and Technology (HST) and
Department of Brain and Cognitive Sciences,
Massachusetts Institute of Technology, USA

"*Drs. Robinson and Thompson's book sheds needed light on the lingering problem
of high illiteracy rates among African American students, especially boys. The book
does far more than identify the problem. The authors of the well-chosen articles,
offer solid suggestions for changes in the way we educate students to provide
instruction that can close the persistent achievement gap, which leaves too many
African American boys with few educational and employment opportunities upon
leaving the PK–12 public school system. Their book is a must-read for educational
administrators, policy makers, and teachers.*"

William Kitz is Associate Director, Project Success,
University of Wisconsin-Oshkosh, USA

Promoting Academic Readiness for African American Males with Dyslexia

This timely book tackles underlying issues that see disproportionate numbers of African American males with dyslexia undiagnosed, untreated, and falling behind their peers in terms of literacy achievement.

Considering factors including dialectic linguistic difference, limited phonological awareness, and the intersectionality of gender, language, and race, the studies included in this volume illustrate how classroom practices at preschool and elementary levels are failing to support students at risk of reading and writing difficulties. *Promoting Academic Readiness for African American Males with Dyslexia* shows that it is possible to provide every girl and boy, and particularly African American boys with effective support and appropriate interventions enabling them to read at a level that is conducive to ongoing academic performance and success. This, argue the authors of this volume, is vital to the social, emotional, moral, and intellectual development of our society.

This edited volume was originally published as a special issue of *Reading & Writing Quarterly: Overcoming Learning Difficulties*. It will be of great interest to graduate and postgraduate students, researchers, and academics in the field of African American Education, Educational Equity, Race studies, Multiple learning difficulties, and Literacy development.

Shawn Anthony Robinson is Senior Research Associate in the Wisconsin's Equity and Inclusion Laboratory (Wei LAB) and an Instructional Program Manager in the Department of Rehabilitation Psychology and Special Education, University of Wisconsin Madison, USA.

Corey Thompson is Associate Professor at Cardinal Stritch University, USA.

Routledge Research in Educational Equality and Diversity

Books in the series include:

British Pakistani Boys, Education and the Role of Religion
In the Land of the Trojan Horse
Karamat Iqbal

Gender in Learning and Teaching
Feminist Dialogues Across International Boundaries
Edited by Carol A. Taylor, Chantal Amade-Escot and Andrea Abbas

Nationality and Ethnicity in an Israeli School
A Case Study of Jewish-Arab Students
Dalya Yafa Markovich

Intersectional Pedagogy
Creative Education Practices for Gender and Peace Work
Gal Harmat

Schools as Queer Transformative Spaces
Global Narratives on Sexualities and Genders
Jón Ingvar Kjaran and Helen Sauntson

Promoting Academic Readiness for African American Males with Dyslexia
Implications for Preschool to Elementary School Teaching
Edited by Shawn Anthony Robinson and Corey Thompson

For more information about this series, please visit: www.routledge.com/ Routledge-Research-in-Educational-Equality-and-Diversity/book-series/ RREED

Promoting Academic Readiness for African American Males with Dyslexia

Implications for Preschool to Elementary School Teaching

Edited by Shawn Anthony Robinson and Corey Thompson

Routledge
Taylor & Francis Group

NEW YORK AND LONDON

First published 2020
by Routledge
605 Third Avenue, New York, NY 10017

and by Routledge
2 Park Square, Milton Park, Abingdon, Oxon, OX14 4RN

First issued in paperback 2021

Routledge is an imprint of the Taylor & Francis Group, an informa business

Publisher's Note
The publisher has gone to great lengths to ensure the quality of this reprint
but points out that some imperfections in the original copies may be
apparent.

Library of Congress Cataloging-in-Publication Data
A catalog record for this book has been requested

ISBN 13: 978-1-03-223967-5 (pbk)
ISBN 13: 978-0-367-41537-2 (hbk)

Typeset in Times New Roman
by Apex CoVantage, LLC

This edited book is dedicated to the scholars, teachers, and parents in the streets and classrooms advocating for early identification and effective literacy instruction for all students, specifically those with dyslexia from underserved communities. More importantly, this publication is devoted to my late professor Dr. Robert T. Nash who taught me how to read at 18 years of age when I started college with an elementary-level education.

Image 0.1 Doctor Dyslexia Dude

Source: Hadnot (2018).

Contents

x *Contents*

Acknowledgments

This edited book would not have been possible without having a strong faith in God, staying encouraged, and understanding the true purpose of how this scholarship has the ability to add a new and much-needed direction to both the discussion of the academic achievement and disparities of African Americans boys with a learning disability (i.e., dyslexia). I am grateful to all the contributing authors with whom I have had the pleasure to work with, and I appreciate their patience throughout the long process. I am especially thankful to the following colleagues for supporting this scholarship and/or providing editorial assistance: Dr. Steve Graham, Dr. Corey Thompson, Dr. Bill Kitz, Dr. Richard McGregory, Dr. Melinda Leko, and Paula Moraine.

However, the original publication of the Special Issue would not have been accomplished without the approval of the *Reading & Writing Quarterly: Overcoming Learning Difficulties* editor Susan Lenski (Portland State University). Dr. Lenski spent countless hours responding to my inquires, providing technical support, and offering leadership when things did not go as I had planned. Next, I'd like to acknowledge Elsbeth Wright, an editor with Taylor & Francis, for inviting me to submit the Special Issues for republication in a book format.

Nobody has been more important to me in the pursuit of this scholarship than my family. I must thank Inshirah (my wife) whose love and guidance are with me in whatever scholarly activity I pursue as well as my sons (Jeremiah and Ezekiel). My family and friends provided unending inspiration and continuously kept me focused on completing the Special Issue that is now turned into an edited book. I am also forever thankful to my mom for her love and guidance.

Prelude

African American boys with dyslexia, and their literacy development

Shawn Anthony Robinson and
Corey Thompson

Academic success for African American boys in Special Education is frequently elusive as the United States continues to endure the legacy of academic discrimination (Blanchett, 2010; Kena et al., 2015). Educational policies have not fully protected the equal rights of students in Special Education, adequately responded to the learning needs of these students' academic shortcomings and have not been leveraged to take advantage of these students' strengths (Robinson, 2017a, 2017b). Further, schools have struggled with assisting African Americans (AA), especially boys, reaching the proficient and advanced reading and writing skills required as they matriculate through the Pre-Kindergarten and Elementary grade levels; this struggle continues to result in lower academic outcomes as these students progress educationally. Thus, the reading gap is widely recognized as an urgent crisis (Parkinson & Rowan, 2008) and evident by Barton and Coley's (2009) assertion:

> Most of the progress in closing the achievement gap in reading and mathematics occurred during the 1970's and 1980's. Since then, overall progress in closing the gaps has slowed. With the exception of the gap in reading for 9-year-olds in 2008, the size of the gaps seen in the late 1980's has never been smaller
>
> (p. 7).

In an effort to make change within the contents of the educational system, the former Obama Administration *Race to the Top Early Learning Challenge Program* raised public awareness for the need for educators to refocus their responsiveness on early childhood learning and academic readiness (Hardman & Dawson, 2008; Wu, Morgan & Farkas, 2014). Regrettably, African American boys were, and continue to be, disproportionately labeled "at risk" for being academically unprepared and received lower academic standards, which continued to widen the reading gap (Aud et al., 2012; Lee, 2008; McCarthy & Morote, 2009).

To date, the scholarly literature on African American boys with dyslexia is limited in scope (Robinson, 2013), which leaves many unanswered questions about the inequality in literacy and language interventions. Lindo (2006) (see *Remedial and Special Education, 27* (3), 148–153) examined 10 years of articles in this area from *Reading Research Quarterly* (1994–2004), the *Journal of Educational Psychology* (1994–2004) and all volumes of the *Journal of Scientific Study of Reading* (1997–2007). Lindo's analysis revealed that none of the research articles reported conclusions by race and suggested that in addition to increasing the quantity of rigorous studies for this population, more reading interventions need to include African American boys (Flowers, 2007; Hoyles & Hoyles, 2010; Proctor, Graves & Esch, 2012).

Robinson, Ford, Harlep, Ellis, (2016) asserted ". . . a focus on prevention and early intervention is essential in order to support these students, their families, and their educators to reduce the special education-to-prison pipeline that is destroying our students, communities, and nation" (p. 3). Early screening, identification and assessments, effective language and literacy instruction, and teaching pedagogy and expectations all have major implications for academic readiness for AA males with dyslexia in preschool–elementary school (Tatum & Muhammad, 2012; Thompson & Shamberger, 2015).

Attaining the necessary reading skills results in a division between those students who meet academic grade level standards and those who may not (Blanchett, Klingner, & Harry, 2009). African American boys continue to perform below proficient level on assessments of early reading, writing, vocabulary, and phonological awareness compared to their White peers. Thus, this gap between African Americans and Whites lingers on through secondary schooling, and boys in particular are at a noticeable risk of experiencing difficulties with reading. This national crisis is not new, as it has been documented for years (de Valenzuela, Copeland, Qi, Park, 2006).

An overview of the reading crisis: a historical perspective

In an historic article titled, "Negro Illiteracy in the United States," Lichtenberger (1913) posited that the rate of illiteracy among people of color throughout the United States (U.S.) was disturbing as their illiteracy rate far exceeded that of Whites. Lichtenberger explained that, prior to the abolishment of slavery, the academic system had a long history of segregation between the rich and poor, and students of different ethnicities (Hurn, 1978).

In fact, it was historically a criminal offense to teach any student of color to read or write, as education was mainly accessible to White students who received private schooling or tutoring.

Students from a lower socioeconomic status were also deprived of a fair and equal education, as well as of curriculum focusing on reading, writing, and math (Sirin, 2005). The neglect for enhancing the quality of human life was manifested by failing to teach students of color, and the result was that the education African Americans received was an act of mercy/generosity of the state. Many Whites did not want colored children to become educated, fearing they would challenge White supremacy and not be content with jobs working in the fields or in domestic service (Woodson, 1933).

In the early education period in the United States, between 1776–1840, formal education with high standards was reserved for those of European ancestry, and "Negroes" were denied equal education. Thus, teaching African Americans to read was considered unimportant rather than urgent, which resulted in the classification of two groups: (1) White students who received rigorous education, and (2) African American students who were prevented from receiving an equal education. At this time, antebellum leaders believed teaching reading to African Americans constituted a threat to the establishment of slavery, as self-knowledge could lead to the pursuit of one's liberation and personal freedom (Butchart, 2010).

These early periods in education in the United States set the stage for our current situation. Illiteracy has continued to be a major hurdle for African Americans, and their lack of access to reading instruction resulted in educational disparities which have spanned the full length of our Nation's history. For instance, in a report published by the U.S. Department of Commerce/ Bureau of the Census, researchers publicized the percent of illiteracy in the population by race from 1870 to 1969 (see Table 0.1), and the data shows persistent disproportion in reading.

The data shown above in the area of reading makes clear the historical legacy and continuing education inequities faced by African Americans, which continue to be encountered today. Fast-forwarding to the 21st century, Lichtenberger's findings are very pertinent as students of color in special education continue to face numerous educational inequities within the academic systems (Connor, 2008).

Literacy in the 21st century: there are still reading discrepancies

When examining the long-lasting impact illiteracy has had on students within the educational system, it is not surprising that African Americans continue to face educational inequalities. This is evidenced by the persistent

Table 0.1 Data for 1870 – 1940 are for the population 10 years old and over; data for 1947, 1952, 1959, and 1969 are for the population 14 years old and over.

Table A: Percent Illiterate in The Population by Race: 1870 To 1969

Year	Total	White	Negro and other races
1969	1.0	0.7	3.6[1]
1959	2.2	1.6	7.5
1952	2.5	1.8	10.2
1947	2.7	1.8	11.0
1940	2.9[2]	2.0[2]	11.5[2]
1930	4.3	3.0	16.4
1920	6.0	4.0	23.0
1910	7.7	5.0	30.5
1900	10.7	6.2	44.5
1890	13.3	7.7	56.8
1880	17.0	9.4	70.0
1870	20.0	11.5	79.9

1 Negro only in 1969
2 Estimated

U.S. Department of Commerce/ Bureau of the Census

racial/ethnic disproportions in reading statistics despite governmental laws aimed at lessening racial discrepancies (Board of Education. v. Rowley, 458 U.S. 176, 1982; Brown v. Board of Education of Topeka, 347 U.S. 483, 1954; Mills v. Board of Education of District of Columbia, 348 F. Supp. 866 (D.D.C. 1972); etc.).

Even with the *Brown V Board of Education* Supreme Court ruling that acknowledged such practices violated the Fourteenth Amendment – section 1 (Ancheta, 2006; O'Connor & Fernandez, 2006; Welner, 2006). It is clear that our educational system has not made sufficient progress in advancing outcomes for African American boys in the area of reading. The Fourteenth Amendment addresses many aspects of the rights of citizens, but given the history of America and slavery, students of color have been deprived of the liberty which results from a free and appropriate education, which has been evident by various legal cases and laws (Albrecht et al., 2011). The inequalities existing in modern times plague student development and may be an immediate result of a history of institutional racism (Leonardo & Grubb, 2013).

Reading gap

First, when analyzing reading trends that include age and race between 1971–1990 shows disparate achievement among African American and White students. For instance, White nine-year-olds' reading performance was very consistent across those years, while the reading scores for African American children of the same age evidenced no change. As a result, little progress was made in closing the reading gap between African American students and their White peers. Moreover, the overall gap between these students was notable (see; U.S. Department of Education, National Center for Education Statistics, National Assessment of Educational Progress).

Second, from 1992–2017 there was persistent disproportionality in reading scores between White and African American fourth grade students. In 1992, 68% of African Americans were reading at rates below basic compared to 29% of their White counterparts; more than twenty years later, the gap is still present. In 2017, 49% of African Americans read below basic compared to 22% of White students National Center for Education Statistics, [NAEP], 2018). The NAEP reading assessment is given every two years to students in grades 4 and 8, and approximately every four years at grade 12 (see NAEP Reading Report Card).

Further, the lack of educational access to high-quality preschools and/ or high academic standards (i.e., reading) has resulted in other disparities, which included but are not limited to African Americans arriving in Pre-K with lower levels of academic readiness than their peers. Hence, over 80% of fourth and eighth grade African American students read below grade level compared to 57% of White students (*The Condition of Education 2015* (NCES 2015–144). For instance, Mol and Bus (2011) asserted students from socially disadvantaged communities are less likely to be exposed to a home environment with rich print, have limited access to those types of environments and other community resources that would assist them in overcoming those reading difficulties. As a potential result, elementary age children from low-income families reputedly hear roughly 30 million fewer words than their peers from more affluent communities. This language or word gap has been linked to deficiencies in third-grade reading skills (Hart & Risley, 1995).

Further, when factoring in reading gaps, the percentage of students with above average reading proficiency scores on statewide reading assessments compared to their White counterparts is abysmal (Schott Foundation for Public Education, 2012). Moreover, the inequalities students of color encounter include additional factors such as lower curriculum standards, cultural-relevant pedagogy, and high stakes testing (Buly & Valencia, 2002; Ladson-Billings, 2012). Arguably, the disproportionality in education for boys of color is not a new phenomenon in America's society. It is a continued societal and chronic challenge in education, which threatens to ravage the futures of those caught in such disparity (Skiba, et al., 2006).

As a consequence, African Americans who also actually have reading disabilities may experience higher rates of disciplinary actions, as a result of being exposed to behavior interventions rather than being offered the necessary academic supports needed to reach their full academic potential (Shifrer, Muller, & Callahan, 2011). Overall, PreK–12 educational policies have not fully protected the equal "educational" rights or adequately responded to remedy African Americans academic shortcomings in the area of reading.

This persistent reading gap has not closed in generations, which is deeply harmful to our American democracy. With every passing year, where problems related to the reading gap have not been alleviated, the damage is costly and no failure is more expensive than the failure to educate our students of color, especially African American males, in the PK–12 years. The danger to our future scholars becomes more critical each year, and these are problems deeply rooted in America. Also, while teachers cannot change the past, we can, and must, change the special education system that shapes the future of African American boys with reading disabilities and dyslexia.

Where are we today: African American boys

Clinicians, educators, scholars, and policymakers have studied racial disparities in education for decades (Fiscella & Kitzman, 2009; Sanders, Federico, Klass, Abrams, Dreyer, 2009), yet these disparities persist at alarming rates (Hair, Hanson, Wolfe, Pollak, 2015). Barriers such as poverty, limited access to healthcare, ineffective clinical and educational practices, disability status, school suspensions, racial bias, disproportionately high rates of reading failure and poor literacy are described in the respective bodies of literature, which widen the achievement gap (Klebanoff & Syme, 2013). Yet, despite the research from various professional disciplines, little progress has been made in decreasing inequalities or closing the noted achievement gap between African American boys and their White counterparts (Newacheck, Stein, Bauman, & Hung, 2003; Robinson, 2018).

It has been well-documented that educational inequalities are greater for African American boys than for any other population, and when disability status is factored in, the risk of academic failure and poor health outcomes is increased compared to White peers (Birru & Steinman, 2004). For young African American boys with a learning disability in reading (i.e., dyslexia), collaboration among disciplines is imperative for understanding the additive effects of these specific barriers on health, development, and education outcomes (Braveman et al., 2011; Weekes, 2012).

When barriers exist and interact in ways that limit access to an appropriate educational diagnosis and subsequent educational services, it is unlikely that African American boys will develop the reading and writing skills needed for success in society today. Low literacy intensifies the difficulties students face in overcoming barriers to health and education services, resulting in a stubbornly high achievement gap and poor health outcomes. Robinson, Ford, Hartlep, and Ellis, (2016) noted that the current imbalance of literature involving African Americans, particularly those with dyslexia, may reflect misunderstandings and misguided practices involving the education of this population; lack of awareness of dyslexia is a potential cause of reading and/or behavior problems and may result in erroneous, inappropriate placement into special education classes for emotional or behavioral disorders. Labeling the student's need as a behavioral one does little to address the root problem, and, in fact, may create unnecessary detrimental consequences over time (Aud, et al., 2012).

Although not specific to African American boys, Ozernov-Palchik & Gaab (2016) recently described what they term the dyslexia paradox, stating that it is, "detrimental to the well-being of children and their families who experience the psychosocial implications of dyslexia for years prior to diagnosis" (2016, p. 157). Moreover, the Yale Center for Dyslexia & Creativity launched the Multicultural Dyslexia Awareness Initiative (YCDC-MDAI) noted that

> While there are numerous curricula and programs designed to improve reading, dyslexia is often overlooked when searching for causes of illiteracy. Even though it is by far the most common reading disability, many of those with dyslexia remain undiagnosed and untreated. This is especially true in public schools and even more so in African-American and Latino communities (para. 2; http://dyslexia.yale.edu/advocacy/ycdc-initiatives/multicultural-outreach/)

Further, the fact that dyslexia remains undiagnosed and untreated not only influences education and health disparities within the minority communities, but are also important areas of examination (Shea, Beers, McDonald, Quistberg, Ravenell, Asch, 2004). From the perspective of addressing literacy related barriers, researchers and clinicians are in a unique position to influence outcomes for individual children and their families well before the age of school entry (Neve & Briers, 2016).

For instance, parents often rely on their child's clinician for information and guidance regarding care for both typical and atypical development (Shonkoff, 2014). Despite a push for early identification and intervention for all children, students from underserved communities, such as African

American boys with dyslexia, are at much higher risk for academic and even health disparities, compared to their White and/or non-disabled peers (Peterson-Besse et al., 2014).

Unfortunately, clinicians have reported less confidence in identification and referrals for children ages three to five years of age (Shah, Kunnavakkam, & Msall, 2013). In addition to examining the limitations within the education systems, studying the interaction among multiple barriers may offer additional understanding for decreasing and preventing the significant disparities for African American boys with dyslexia. Arguably, this represents one of the most pressing social justice issues in America. Therefore, developing a body of literature specifically addressing the impact of interactions among gender, race, and dyslexia in education is the necessary first step to preventing the negative sequelae that perpetuate academic failure, poor health, and underachievement in this underserved population (Spangler, 2016).

Synopsis of edited book

To address the reading discrepancies affecting countless number of African American boys with dyslexia in the 21st century, this edited book synthesizes current research related to not only language and literacy interventions, but also sheds light on promoting academic readiness and calls for a bold new vision for reading and writing intervention(s) (Cooper et al., 2015; Handler, 2016; Robinson, 2019; Robinson & Robinson, 2018). The original publication of these manuscripts in this edited book were printed in a 2019 special issue titled Promoting Academic Readiness for African American Males with Dyslexia: Teaching Implications for Preschool-Elementary School in *Reading & Writing Quarterly: Overcoming Learning Difficulties* 35(1)[1] (see Robinson & Thompson, 2019).

To begin, in her introduction titled "The Forgotten Boys", Maryanne Wolf sets the stage for this needed area of scholarship, describes her experiences in the reading field, discusses the significance of this research, and ends her position with ". . . I don't care what diagnosis is given, as long as every girl and boy – particularly African American boys, who have been long neglected – can receive intervention that will propel them to read at a level that will release their potential to become productive human beings in our society" (p.3).

In chapter one, titled "How Does a Metalinguistic Phonological Intervention Impact the Reading Achievement and Language of African American Boys?" authors Russell and Shiffler document results from a reading intervention designed to alleviate the effects of vernacular differences and phonological awareness among African American boys who were placed in two groups: low phonological awareness and average phonological awareness. The intervention lasted 4-weeks, which included phonemic techniques targeting final consonant patterns with an emphasis on a metacognitive understanding of phonological differences between African American English and academic English.

Through statistical analysis, their study provided several recommendations for teachers to increase phonological awareness abilities for students identified as having reading difficulties. For instance, similar to the policy recommendations above, the authors suggested that teachers consider implementing explicit and direct instruction in conjunction with phonemic manipulation and verbal scaffolding related to a metacognitive understanding of the phonological differences between African American English and academic English.

In the second chapter, titled "Reading and Language Performance of Low-Income, African American Boys in Grades 1 – 5" authors Washington, Branum-Martin, Lee-James, and Sun examined the gender gap in language and reading skills in a sample of low income African American boys compared to African American girls from the same neighborhoods and schools. Researchers used three different statistical analyses to gauge the reading and language performance of the participants in the following areas: 1) language 2) letter-word identification, 3) passage comprehension, 4) decoding, 5) reading fluency, 6) reading vocabulary, and 7) cognition.

Their results offered a variety of outcomes. First, there was no difference in performance on language or intelligence measures between boys and girls at any grade level. Second, similar to the research of Matthews, Kizzie, Rowley, and Cortina (2010) and Bouchamma, Poulin, and Ruel (2014), authors found that that there was a significant difference in reading skills by gender (girls) in fourth and fifth grades. Third, authors discovered no differences in growth trajectories of either gender for language or intelligence but found a change in passage comprehension and reading fluency, which favored girls on passage comprehension. Furthermore, on reading fluency, boys showed major deceleration at fifth grade. Overall, authors provided recommendations to support the literacy and language development of African American boys and their reading achievement.

In the third chapter, titled "Exploring the Master Narrative: Racial Knowledge and Understanding of Language and Literacy Pedagogy for Special Education Teacher Candidates" authors Bank and Gibson follow the scholarship of authors Russell and Shiffler, and Washington, Branum-Martin, Lee-James, and Sun by exploring the role of African American English but focus on teacher training programs. Authors offer a conceptual framework that can be used as a pedological tool in helping preservice teachers understand the historical intersectionality of race, gender, and language when instructing African American boys. Overall, their framework may continue a needed dialogue on variables impacting the gloomy academic achievement and disproportionality in special education among African American boys, and the instructional and characters of African American English, which can influence their literacy and language attainment.

In the fourth and final chapter, titled "Teaching Writing to Young African American Male Students Using Evidence-Based Practices" authors, Graham, Harris and Beard reanalyzed the statistics from five true-experiments conducted with African American students experiencing dysgraphia. Thus, the reexamined studies had taught the fundamental writing process or skill through the use of evidenced-based writing practices that has been validated in previous studies (See MacArthur, Graham, & Fitzgerald, 2008). Those six strategies, at the core of evidenced-based writing practices called Self-Regulated Strategy Development, incorporate: (1) developing background knowledge, (2) discussing it, (3) modeling it, (4) supporting it, (5) memorizing it, and (6) independent performing the writing task. Therefore, the authors found that in the studies teaching the fundamental writing processes and skills using evidence-based practices, results showed the approach improved African American boys writing abilities, even when writing or reading skills were not directly taught.

In conclusion, as co-editors, we are pleased to share this edited book with the hope that the articles are used to help improve the learning of African American boys with dyslexia in preschool through elementary school. As Wolf (2019) asserted, this specific student population has been neglected for far too long, something Lindo (2006) and other scholars have pointed out, and this neglect results in numerous and extensive gaps in knowledge, theory, and academic support. Thus, we are aware that this edited book neither fills *all* voids nor meets *all* needs. Nonetheless, the chapters have much to offer in the field of Language and Literacy and beyond. Preschool through elementary school teachers must be responsive to African American boys with dyslexia, and a focus on prevention and early intervention is essential in order to support these students, their families, and their educators to reduce the noted reading discrepancies that are destroying our students, communities, and nation.

Note

1 The chapters in this edited book are not in the same order as in the Special Issues.

References

Albrecht, S. F., Skiba, R. J., Losen, D. J., Chung, C. G., & Middelberg, L. (2011). Federal policy on disproportionality in special education: Is it moving us forward? *Journal of Disability Policy Studies, 23*, 14–25.

Ancheta, A. N. (2006). Civil rights, education research, and the courts. *Educational Researcher, 35*(1), 26–29.

Aud, S., Hussar, W., Johnson, F., Kena, G., Roth, E., Manning, E., Wang, X., & Zhang, J. (2012). *The condition of education 2012* (NCES 2012–045). U.S. Department of Education, National Center for Education Statistics. Washington, DC. Retrieved from http://nces.ed.gov/pubs2012/2012045.pdf

Barton, P. E., & Coley, R. J. (2009). *Parsing the achievement gap II : Policy information report.* Princeton, NJ: Educational Testing Service. Retrieved from http://www.ets.org/Media/Research/pdf/PICPARSINGII.pdf

Birru M, & Steinman R. A (2004). Online health information and low-literacy African Americans. *Journal of Medical Internet Research. 6*(3): e26.

Blanchett, W. J. (2010). Telling it like it is: The role of race, class, & culture in the perpetuation of learning disability as a privileged category for the White middle class. *Disability Studies Quarterly, 30*(2), 6.

Blanchett, W. J., Klingner, J. K., & Harry, B. (2009). The intersection of race, culture, language, and disability: Implications for urban education. *Urban Education, 44*(4), 389–409.

Board of Education. v. Rowley, 458 U.S. 176, 1982.

Bouchamma, Y., Poulin, V., & Ruel, C. (2014). Impact of reading strategy use on girls' and boys' achievement. *Reading Psychology, 35*(4), 312–331.

Braveman, P. A., Kumanyika, S., Fielding, J., LaVeist, T., Borrell, L. N., Manderscheid, R., & Troutman, A. (2011). Health Disparities and Health Equity: The Issue Is Justice. *American Journal of Public Health, 101*(S1), S149–55.

Brown v. Board of Education of Topeka, 347 U.S. 483, 1954.

Buly, M. R., & Valencia, S. W. (2002). Below the bar: Profiles of students who fail state reading assessments. *Educational Evaluation and Policy Analysis, 24*(3), 219–239.

Butchart, Ronald E. (2010). *Schooling the freed people: teaching, learning, and the struggle for Black freedom, 1861–1876.* Chapel Hill: University of North Carolina.

Connor, D. J. (2008). *Urban narratives: Portraits in progress life at the intersections of learning disability, race, and social class.* New York, NY: Peter Lang.

Cooper, L. A., Ortega, A. N., Ammerman, A. S., Buchwald, D., Paskett, E. D., Powell, L. H.,. . . Williams, D. R. (2015). Calling for a Bold New Vision of Health Disparities Intervention Research. *American Journal of Public Health,* 105, S374–6.

de Valenzuela, J. S., Copeland, S. R., Qi, C. H., Park, M. (2006). Examining educational equity: Revisiting the disproportionate representation of minority students in special education. *Exceptional Children, 72*(4), 425–441.

Fiscella, K., & Kitzman, H. (2009). Disparities in Academic Achievement and Health: The Intersection of Child Education and Health Policy. *Pediatrics, 123*(3), 1073–1080.

Flowers, L. A. (2007), Recommendations for Research to Improve Reading Achievement for African American Students. Reading Research Quarterly, 42: 424–428. doi:10.1598/RRQ.42.3.8

Graham, S., MacArthur, C. A., & Fitzgerald, J. (2013). *Best practices in Writing Instruction.* New York: The Guilford Press.

Hadnot, B. (2018). *Doctor dyslexia dude* [Illustrator]. https://drdyslexiadude.com

Hair, N. L., Hanson, J. L., Wolfe, B. L., & Pollak, S. D. (2015). Association of Child Poverty, Brain Development, and Academic Achievement. *JAMA Pediatrics*, *169*(9), 822–829.

Handler, S. M. (2016). Dyslexia. Contemporary Pediatrics, *33*(8), 18–23.

Hardman, M.L. & Dawson, S. (2008, winter). The impact of federal public policy on curriculum & instruction for students with disabilities in the general classroom. *Preventing School Failure*, *52*(2), 5–11.

Hart, B., & Risley, T. R. (1995). *Meaningful differences in the everyday experience of young American children*. Paul H Brookes Publishing.

Hoyles, A. & Hoyles, M. (2010) Race and dyslexia. *Race Ethnicity and Education*, *13*(2), 209–231.

Hurn, C. J. (1978). *The limits and possibilities of schooling: An introduction to the sociology of education*. Boston: Allyn and Bacon.

Kena, G., Musu-Gillette, L., Robinson, J., Wang, X., Rathbun, A., Zhang, J., Wilkinson-Flicker, S., Barmer, A., and Dunlop Velez, E. (2015). *The Condition of Education 2015* (NCES 2015–144). U.S. Department of Education, National Center for Education Statistics. Washington, DC. Retrieved [August 16th, 2018] from http://nces.ed.gov/pubsearch.

Klebanoff C, A., & Syme, S. L. (2013). Education: A Missed Opportunity for Public Health Intervention. *American Journal of Public Health*, 103(6), 997–1001. https://doi-org.ezproxy.library.wisc.edu/10

Ladson-Billings, G. (2012). Through a glass darkly: The persistence of race in education research & scholarship. *Educational Researcher*, *41*(4), 115–120.

Lee, C. D. (2008). Synthesis of research on the role of culture in learning among African American youth: The contributions of Asa G. Hilliard, III. *Review of Educational Research*, *78*(4), 797–827.

Leonardo, Z., & Grubb, W. N. (2013). *Racism and education*. Taylor & Francis.

Lichtenberger, J. P. (1913). Negro Illiteracy in the United States. *The Annals of the American Academy of Political and Social Science*, *49*(1), 177–185.

Lindo, E. J. (2006). The African American presence in reading intervention experiments. *Remedial and Special Education*, *27*(3), 148–153.

McCarthy, P. B., & Morote, E. (2009). The link between investment in early childhood preschools and high school graduation rates for African American males in the United States of America. *Contemporary Issues in Early Childhood*, *10*(3), 232–239.

Matthews, J. S., Kizzie, K. T., Rowley, S. J., & Cortina, K. (2010). African Americans and boys: Understanding the literacy gap, tracing academic trajectories, and evaluating the role of learning-related skills. *Journal of Educational Psychology*, *102*, 757–771. doi:10.1037/a0019616.

Mills v. Board of Education of District of Columbia, 348 F. Supp. 866 (D.D.C. 1972).

Mol, S. E., & Bus, A. G. (2011). To read or not to read: a meta-analysis of print exposure from infancy to early adulthood. *Psychological bulletin*, *137*(2), 267.

National Center for Education Statistics. (2018). *National Assessment of Educational Progress: An overview of NAEP*. Washington, D.C.: National Center for Education Statistics, Institute of Education Sciences, U.S. Dept. of Education.

Newacheck, P. W.; Stein, R. E.; Bauman, L.; & Hung, Y. (2003). Disparities in the prevalence of disability between black and white children. *Archives of Pediatrics and Adolescent Medicine, 157*(3), 244–248.

Neve, J., & Briers, G. (2016). Reducing inequities in health and life expectancy. *Nursing Times, 112*(5):12–4.

O'Connor, C., & Fernandez, S. D. (2006). Race, class, and disproportionality: Reevaluating the relationship between poverty and special education placement. *Educational Researcher, 35*(6), 6–11.

Ozernov-Palchik, O., & Gaab, N. (2016). Tackling the 'dyslexia paradox': reading brain and behavior for early markers of developmental dyslexia. *Wiley Interdisciplinary Reviews: Cognitive Science, 7*(2), 156–176.

Parkinson, J., & Rowan, B. (2008). Poverty, early literacy achievement, and education reform. In S. B. Neuman (Ed.) *Educating the other America: Top experts tackle poverty, literacy, and achievement in our schools* (pp. 73–90). Baltimore, MD: Brookes.

Peterson-Besse, J. J., Walsh, E. S., Horner-Johnson, W., Goode, T. D., & Wheeler, B. (2014). Barriers to health care among people with disabilities who are members of underserved racial/ethnic groups: a scoping review of the literature. *Medical care, 52*, S51-S63.

Proctor, S.L., Graves, S. L., & Esch, R. C. (2012). Assessing African American students for specific learning disabilities: The promises and perils of response of intervention. *Journal of Negro Education, 81*(3), 268–282.

Robinson, S. A. (2019). Critical Literacy Impacts African American Boys' Reading Identity. *Gifted Child Today, 42*(3), 150–156.

Robinson, S. A. (2018). *Untold Narratives: African Americans who received Special Education services and succeeded beyond expectations.* Charlotte, NC: Information Age Publishing.

Robinson, S. A. (2017a). Intersection of Race, Giftedness and Dyslexia: Triple Identity Theory. *Advanced Development – a Journal on Adult Giftedness, 16*, 78–94.

Robinson, S. A. (2017b). Phoenix Rising: An Auto-Ethnographic Account of a Gifted Black Male with Dyslexia. *Journal for the Education of the Gifted*, 1–7.

Robinson, S. A. (2013). Educating Black males with dyslexia. *Interdisciplinary Journal of Teaching and Learning, 3*(3), 159–174.

Robinson, S. A., & Robinson, I. V. (2018). Doctor Dyslexia Dude. Self-published. ISBN # 978-1-7323349-0-8

Robinson, S. A., & Thompson, C. L. (2019). Promoting Academic Readiness for African American males with dyslexia: Teaching Implications for Preschool-Elementary School. *Reading and Writing Quarterly, 35*(1), p. 1–64.

Robinson, S. A, Ford, D.Y., Hartlep, N., & Ellis, A. L. (2016). African American males with learning disabilities in special education throughout the P-20 educational pipeline. *Journal of African American Males in Education, 7*(1).

Sanders, L. M., Federico, S., Klass, P., Abrams, M., & Dreyer, B. (2009). Literacy and Child Health: A Systematic Review. *Archives of Pediatrics and Adolescent Medicine, 163*(2):131–140.

Schott Foundation for Public Education. (2012). The urgency of now: The Schott 50 state report on public education and Black males. Retrieved from http://www. blackboysreport.org/ urgency-of-now.pdf

Shah, R. P., Kunnavakkam, R., & Msall, M. E. (2013). Pediatricians' knowledge, attitudes, and practice patterns regarding special education and individualized education programs. *Academic pediatrics, 13*(5), 430–435.

Shea J. A., Beers B. B., McDonald V.J., Quistberg D.A., Ravenell K.L., & Asch D.A. (2004). Assessing Health Literacy in African American and Caucasian Adults: Disparities in Rapid Estimate of Adult Literacy in Medicine (REALM) Scores. *Health Literacy and Family Medicine, 36*(8), 575–581.

Shifter, D., Muller, C., & Callahan, R (2011). "Disproportionality and Learning Disabilities: Passing Apart Race, Socioeconomic Status, and Language." *Journal of Learning Disabilities* 44: 246–257. doi:10.1177/0022219410374236.

Shonkoff, J. P. (2014). Changing the narrative for early childhood investment. *JAMA pediatrics, 168*(2), 105–106

Sirin, S. R. (2005). Socioeconomic status and academic achievement: A meta-analytic review of research. *Review of educational research, 75*(3), 417–453.

Skiba, R. J., Poloni-Staudinger, L., Gallini, S., Simmons, A. B., & Feggins-Azziz, R. (2006). Disparate access: The disproportionality of African American students with disabilities across educational environments. *Council for Exceptional Children, 72*(4), 411–424.

Spangler, M. (2016). 5 steps for assessing dyslexia from a reading specialist. Contemporary Pediatrics, 33(8), 26–27.

Tatum, A. W., & Muhammad, G. E. (2012). African American Males and Literacy Development in Contexts That are Characteristically Urban. *Urban Education, 47*(2), 434–463.

The Yale Center for Dyslexia & Creativity (2019). Retrieved from http://dyslexia.yale.edu

Thompson, G., L. and Shamberger, C., T. (2015) "The Gift That Can Save Lives: Teaching Black Students to Become Good Readers," *Journal of Research Initiatives, 1*(3), 1–10.

U.S. Department of Education, National Center for Education Statistics, National Assessment of Educational Progress (NAEP), *NAEP 2012 Trends in Academic Progress*; and 2012 NAEP Long-Term Trend Reading Assessment. Retrieved summer 2019.

Weekes, CV. (2012). African Americans and health literacy: A systematic review. *ABNF Journal.* 23(4), 76–80.

Welner, K. G. (2006). K–12 race-conscious student assignment policies: Law, social science, and diversity. *Review of Educational Research, 76*(3), 349–382.

Wolf, M. (2019). The Forgotten Boys: Introduction to Special Issue. *Reading and Writing Quarterly, 35*(1), p. 1–3.

Woodson, C. G., *1875–1950. (1933). The mis-education of the Negro. Washington, D.C.: Associated Publishers.*

Wu, Q., Morgan, P. L., & Farkas, G. (2014). Does Minority Status Increase the Effect of Disability Status on Elementary Schoolchildren's Academic Achievement? *Remedial and Special Education, 35*(6), 366–377.

"The forgotten boys"
Introduction to the special issue

Maryanne Wolf

Jeanne Chall, one of the greatest reading scholars of the 20th century, directed the Harvard Reading Lab and conducted the most comprehensive investigation of reading methods ever attempted Chall (1967, 1983). More than 50 years ago, she provided compelling evidence supporting the use of explicit phonics-based methods of teaching, particularly for struggling readers, whatever the source of the struggle. Chall wanted the study of reading to be based on science and an unflinching assessment of what would give all children, particularly underserved children, their best shot at contributing their talent to society. Shortly before she died, she called me. In retrospect, I believe she knew that she would not live much longer and wanted to propel me and others to work for the children who needed it most. I am introducing this entire special issue with Jeanne Chall, because her last words to me are the cornerstone of the work represented in these pages. In a voice that was halting but adamant, she insisted that the most important issue in American education was to address the problems underlying the reading failure of African American boys, particularly fourth-grade boys. She said it was key to changing education.

In this issue, "Promoting Academic Readiness for African American Males With Dyslexia: Teaching Implications for Preschool–Elementary School," the authors (Washington, Branum-Martin, Lee-James, & Sun; Russell & Shiffler; Banks & Gibson; Graham, Harris, & Beard) describe the sobering, unchanged details that buttress Jeanne Chall's admonition almost 20 years later. As is described in more detail in this volume, African American boys are overrepresented on multiple dimensions of reading failure, poor grades, dropout rates, and school suspensions. It is very important to note that, just as Jeanne worried, only a small percentage of African American boys are proficient in reading at Grade 3. Indeed, all too many are three grades behind in reading by fourth grade, the Maginot Line when fluency is assumed; the materials to be read have become more complex; and few teachers have been trained to deal with reading acquisition or its failure to develop (see Wolf, 2007, 2016, 2018).

But Jeanne described something else that is central to this special issue that has haunted me to this day. I paraphrase only slightly. She told everyone who would listen that if you were poor, Black, and failing, you were doomed to school failure, but if you were middle class, White, and failing, you were likely to be classified as having a learning disability or dyslexia and entitled to intervention. Shawn Anthony Robinson, PhD, the co-editor of this special issue, helped to begin what should never have been needed as a new direction of research: research on the simple fact that there is an entire group of children who are African American, male, and gifted and have dyslexia – largely undiagnosed and usually untreated (Hoyles & Hoyles, 2010; Robinson, 2016; Robinson, 2013). Distinguishing, disentangling, and attending to each of these characteristics and its effects on individuals and society is part of the charge of this special issue.

It could not be more important. One of the statements that preceded this special issue and underscores its urgency is found in Robinson, Ford, Hartlep, and Ellis (2016), who stated, "A focus on prevention and early intervention is essential to support these students, their families, and their educators to reduce the special education-to-prison pipeline that is destroying our students, communities, and nation" (p. 3). The most depressing professional meeting I ever attended took place in a Phoenix office of the Bureau of Prisons where I learned that Arizona – like many other U.S. states – projects the number of prison beds it will need in the future based on third-grade reading failure. This is the pipeline that Robinson and his coauthors asked us to confront as researchers, as educators, as citizens. We cannot progress as a nation if, as Chall recognized, we do not confront and redress reading failure and the multiple reasons for failure in this essential part of our American society.

As illustrated in the articles that follow, many factors, some linguistic and some nonlinguistic, underlie the cycle of reading failure for African American boys. Jeannette Russell and Molly Drake Shiffler focus on linguistic factors that have been the center of sometimes controversial but always needed attention. Specifically, they focus on the effects of dialect differences between academic English and African American English (one of several nonmainstream American English dialects) on phonological processing abilities like phoneme awareness, one of the best-known predictors of reading achievement and dyslexia (Wolf, 2007, 2016). All forms of dyslexia involve reading failure, but not all forms of reading failure involve dyslexia. Understanding the nature and role of dialect differences in reading ability, reading disability, and dyslexia is an underresearched area that requires far more intensive and expanded study.

For example, Shade (2012), a former member of my lab whose dissertation research was supervised by me and Julie Washington, found both phoneme-based and morphosyntactic differences associated with reading failure, a finding that replicated earlier work by Washington. Russell and Shiffler provide a new slant on this direction of research by reporting on a short-term intervention based on explicit metacognitive phoneme–grapheme training that addressed specific dialect differences. Their article both highlights the promise of such interventions and demonstrates the need for more intensive, developmentally based approaches.

Intervention and its importance are also addressed in the article by Steve Graham, Karen R. Harris, and Keith Beard in an area that is also largely neglected: the efficacy of writing interventions for African American males. Reasons for this neglect may spring from the intrinsic untidiness of investigating any topic in which race, gender, socioeconomic conditions, and language use are involved. The authors of this article, and indeed the authors of the entire special issue, dive into this untidiness with rigor and no small courage, emerging with fresh insights into what educators and policymakers should do about the facts on the ground. The disparities in writing between girls and boys, and between African Americans and other children, are some of those facts that need to be examined and changed. Within this context, Graham, Harris, and Beard disaggregate data from five previous interventions on writing and find that the use of evidence-based writing instruction that incorporated known strategies for planning, revising, sentence construction, spelling, handwriting, and self-regulation improved the writing performance of African American males who were having difficulties in writing. These authors' guidelines for teachers provide an important dimension for changing the trajectories of these students.

Joy Banks and Simone Gibson add a slightly different approach to the special issue, but their research is important in the area of teacher preparation. The role of preservice instruction in helping teachers understand how race, gender, and language intersect is critical in these trajectories, as reflected in the article by Banks and Gibson. Although their article may seem to be describing a nonlinguistic factor related to understanding and ameliorating the reading gap among African American boys, these authors in fact return us to the issue of dialect differences and the way in which teachers' attitudes toward African American English can prove a very important ingredient in providing children with culturally responsive teaching. Their conclusions underscore how an understanding of the bi-dialecticism of our students, particularly our male students, provides an essential aspect of preservice training.

Julie A. Washington, Lee Branum-Martin, Ryan Lee-James, and Congying Sun tackle an enormous set of issues in their landmark longitudinal study of language and reading skills among African American boys and girls from first to fifth grades. They find no gender differences in this large accelerated cohort design for language and cognition. Rather, they pinpoint in fourth-grade boys the "beginning of a gap in performance by gender (and SES) that will continue to widen" in reading fluency and comprehension. Further and very important, they illumine how weaknesses in fifth-grade word identification, comprehension, and vocabulary seal the fate of these boys to involve them in a cycle of learning failure from then on. The authors conclude that these trends demonstrate how "these boys simply have developed weak overall reading skills that catch up with them in later grades; reading comprehension and fluency become casualties of these weaknesses." These conclusions pinpoint both where and when things go wrong and in so doing provide a pathway for redressing these weaknesses through explicit instruction in those areas.

Jeanne Chall and the authors of this special issue describe different aspects of the daily realities of the many children who, through no fault of their own, come to school with the odds stacked against them and, often as not, leave school the same way. Perhaps no child has more of these impeding odds than the African American male who is failing to learn to read with no one knowing whether the cause is dyslexia or any of the multiple factors that could result in the same reading behaviors and the same negative social-emotional sequelae that accompany them.

Let me end this introduction with a statement that may surprise readers familiar with my past research on the importance of diagnosing dyslexia. I don't care what diagnosis is given, as long as every girl and boy – particularly African American boys, who have been long neglected – can receive intervention that will propel them to read at a level that will release their potential to become productive human beings in our society. Democracy requires it. The social, emotional, moral, intellectual development of our species needs it. This special issue pushes us one long-needed step closer.

References

Chall, J. S. (1967). *Learning to read: The great debate*. New York: McGraw Hill.

Chall, J. S. (1983). *Stages of reading development*. New York: McGraw-Hill.

Hoyles, A., & Hoyles, M. (2010). Race and dyslexia. *Race Ethnicity and Education*, *13*(2), 209–231.

Robinson, S. A. (2013). Educating black males with dyslexia. *Interdisciplinary Journal of Teaching and Learning*, *3*(3), 159–174.

Robinson, S. A. (2016). Remediating the learning disabilities of black males: Implications for PK–12 teaching. *Journal of Education and Development in the Caribbean*, *15*(1), 159–173.

Robinson, S. A., Ford, D. Y., Hartlep, N., & Ellis, A. L. (2016). African American males with learning disabilities in special education throughout the P-20 educational pipeline. *Journal of African American Males in Education, 7*(1).

Shade, C. V. (2012). An examination of the relationship between morphosyntactic and phonological nonstandard dialect features and literacy skills among African-American children (Doctoral Dissertation). Retrieved from ProQuest Dissertations and These Database. (UMI 3541854).

Wolf, M. (2007). *Proust and the squid: The story and science of the reading brain.* New York: HarperCollins.

Wolf, M. (2016). *Tales of literacy for the 21st Century.* London: Oxford University Press.

Wolf, M. (2018). *Reader, come home: The reading brain in a digital world.* New York: HarperCollins.

1 How does a metalinguistic phonological intervention impact the reading achievement and language of African American boys?

Jeannette Russell and Molly Drake Shiffler

African American (AA) students in low-income areas face systemic educational inequities that contribute to an opportunity gap (Ladson-Billings, 2006) with Euro-American students (i.e., students whose families are of European descent). One result is disparity in literacy achievement resulting from multiple factors, possibly including dialectic linguistic differences between academic English (AE) and African American English (AAE), a form of nonmainstream American English (NMAE; Craig, Zhang, Hensel, & Quinn, 2009). This disparity in reading achievement is evident in the results of 2014–2015 statewide testing in the Midwestern state where the present study was conducted (Wisconsin Department of Public Instruction, 2016), a state that consistently reports one of the widest AA/Euro-American reading achievement gaps in the country (Richards, 2016). Although a state average of 51.7% of all third-grade students, including 60% of White students, scored at the proficient and advanced reading levels, only 19.8% of Black or AA third graders' results registered at these levels (Wisconsin Department of Public Instruction, 2016). Because multiple factors relating to reading acquisition are intertwined, and no one factor alone can account for the low reading performance of AA students, the current study more specifically examined possible relationships between dialectic linguistic differences, phonological awareness abilities, and the results of an intervention targeting the literacy achievement gap.

African American boys specifically are overrepresented on measures of school failure such as reading achievement, failing grades, high school dropout rates, special education assignment, expulsions, and even preschool-level suspensions (Bacon, Banks, Young, & Jackson, 2007; Baker, Cameron, Rimm-Kaufman, & Grissmer, 2012). Compared to 38% of Euro-American boys nationally, only 12% of AA fourth-grade boys are proficient in reading on the National Assessment of Educational Progress (Educational Testing Service, 2011). Thus, AA boys may be three full years behind their peers by the time they enter fourth grade (Educational Testing Service, 2011). Therefore, researchers are currently investigating the factors that have caused the low reading success among AA boys.

Nonlinguistic factors, such as teacher bias (Bacon et al., 2007), poverty (McWayne, Owsianik, Green, & Fantuzzo, 2008), parental involvement (Mangino, 2009), school readiness (Joe & Davis, 2009), and culturally unresponsive teaching (Bacon et al., 2007), may affect the academic success of AA boys. In addition, researchers have examined linguistic factors related to reading achievement differences within pragmatic, syntactic, semantic, morphological, and phonological parameters. Linguistic factors impacting reading achievement also encompass a range of cognitive processes, including phonological processing abilities, which are prominently referenced in the literature on specific reading disabilities or dyslexia. For the purpose of this study, dyslexia is defined as significant difficulty in learning to read that affects fluent word reading and spelling (Duff et al., 2014; Odegard, Ring, Smith, Biggan, & Black, 2008). There is limited research on the implementation of reading achievement intervention programs that address specific factors such as dialectic and phonological processing differences for AA boys.

In a previous study that included both male and female first graders, Russell (2015) implemented a 4-week metalinguistic phonologically-based intervention using diverse quantitative and qualitative measures of reading achievement, phonological awareness, and language variation. The current article describes an analysis of the data obtained from the previous study (Russell, 2015) when iterated only for male students assigned to two groups of phonological proficiency based on results on the Comprehensive Test of Phonological Processing–Second Edition (CTOPP–2; Wagner, Torgesen, Rashotte, & Pearson, 2013) Elision subtest. The purpose of the current analysis was to examine the effects of providing explicit instruction using a metalinguistic, phonological flexibility-based (phoneme–grapheme mapping) intervention for first-grade boys who were speakers of AAE with average or below-average phonological awareness abilities.

Factors in the literacy achievement of AA boys

The president and founder of the Children's Defense Fund, Marian Wright Edelman, examined the challenges facing AA boys and offered strategic guidelines to help them realize their full potential (Educational Testing Service, 2011). Her investigations concluded that schools play a critical role in changing the trajectory of AA boys and should implement improvements to narrow the achievement gap. These improvements include revisiting assessments, setting high expectations, seeking student input, teaching study skills and techniques, engaging community resources, and revamping the curriculum (Educational Testing Service, 2011). Educators may need to further examine how factors such as linguistic differences of speakers of AAE interact with literacy acquisition variables, including phonological processing abilities, to understand the nature of curriculum revision and creation needed to promote AA boys' robust reading development.

Lee (2005) hypothesized that there is a heavier cognitive load on the mental capacity to input print into short-term memory for NMAE speakers because more circuit repetitions and backtracks are needed to resolve the phonological, orthographic, and semantic differences with AE. *Cognitive load* refers to the mental capacity it may take for readers to engage short-term memory when recognizing or sounding out words (Lee, 2005). Mark Seidenberg (personal correspondence, March 10, 2011) has suggested that, because of the phonological mismatch between AAE and AE, speakers of AAE are required to make more ambiguous semantic and orthographic choices between words, which increases cognitive load (or short-term memory demands) during word recognition. Speakers of AAE may have to invest a great deal more effort and attention in decoding words, which results in restricted fluency and ability to make sense of what they are reading.

For students who have phonological processing difficulty in addition to dialectic differences, decoding words requires even more effort and attention, which further restricts fluency and comprehension. In this instance, there is a heavier cognitive load on the mental capacity to input print into short-term memory because more circuit repetitions and backtracks are needed to resolve the phonological, orthographic, and semantic differences between AAE and AE (Lee, 2005). Further exploring the possible compounding influence on literacy acquisition of phonological deficits for speakers of AAE, the three following sections discuss dialectic differences between AAE and AE, phonological processing related to dyslexia, and relevant intervention design research.

Dialectic linguistic differences/oral language of AAE

When educational researchers have investigated the salient factors in the reading success of AA students, the role of AAE has been a focus (Craig, Thompson, Washington, & Potter, 2003; Terry & Connor, 2010; Terry, Connor, Petscher, & Conlin, 2012; Washington & Craig, 1994). AAE is one form of NMAE spoken by predominantly AAs that has its own set of grammatical features and rules (Rickford & Rickford, 2000). The language used by teachers and students in the academic setting is sometimes referred to as AE. Several distinct morphosyntactic and phonological features of AAE differ from AE and may compromise decoding, encoding,

Table 1.1 Phonological features of child and adult African American English.

Definition	Example

Postvocalic consonant reduction
  Deletion of consonant singles
  following vowels
	mouth for /mou/

"g" dropping in final word position Substitutions of /-ng/ for /n/	*waiting* for /waitin'/
Substituting /th/ with /f/ or /d/	*this* for /dis/, *birthday* for /birfday/

Devoicing final consonants
  Voiceless consonants substitute for
  voiced following the vowel
	/his/ for /hiz/

Consonant cluster reduction	*world* for /worl/
Consonant cluster movement	*escape* for /eksape/

Note: Adapted from "Phonological Features of Child African American English," by H. Craig, C. Thompson, J. Washington, & S. Potter, 2003, *Journal of Speech, Language, and Hearing Research, 46*, pp. 626–627. Copyright 2003 by American Speech-Language-Hearing Association. Used with permission.

and comprehension. When sentences have both morphological and syntactic features, the relationship between those features is morphosyntactic. Morphosyntactic features of AAE include omission of the possessive *s, ed*, and linking verb copula; subject expression; indefinite article; third-person singular s; and plural s (Fogel & Ehri, 2006; Washington & Craig, 1994). Another parameter of language is phonology, which is the sound structure of spoken words (Parker & Riley, 2005). AAE has at least nine unique phonological features; examples related to this study are described in Table 1.1. One common distinctive phonological feature of AAE is the deletion of final consonant clusters or blends (Haynes & Moran, 1989; Moran, 1993). The current study's intervention targeted final consonants and consonant clusters with both phonological manipulation and metacognitive dialect-shifting explanation.

Phonological processing abilities in relation to dyslexia

Phonological deficits are cited as the prominent component associated with dyslexia (Blomert & Willems, 2010) according to the research definition adopted by the National Institutes of Health and International Dyslexia Association:

Dyslexia is a specific learning disability that is neurological in origin. It is characterized by difficulty with accurate and/or fluent word recognition and by poor spelling and decoding abilities. These difficulties typically result from a deficit in the phonological component of language that is often unexpected in relation to other cognitive abilities.

(Lyon, Shaywitz, & Shaywitz, 2003, p. 2)

Although not all struggling readers meet the criteria for dyslexia used in schools, the role of phonological processing may still warrant consideration because of its potential role in causing reading difficulties (Blomert & Willems, 2010). In this study, a *phonological deficit* is defined as a decreased ability to discriminate, remember, and manipulate speech sounds in spoken words (Joly-Pottuz, Mercier, Leynaud, & Habib, 2008). Children who have poor phonological awareness skills struggle learning to read and write (Blomert & Willems, 2010). Phonemic decoding of print may be compromised when children are recoding graphemes to phonemes to identify words and consequently determine their meaning. Several studies have revealed a strong link between phonological awareness and early performance in reading and spelling (Ehri, 1997; Juel, Griffith, & Gough, 1986; Treiman, 1994). The capacity to learn correspondences between phonemes and graphemes is essential to achieving efficient reading (Stanovich, 1988). Phonemic training linked to letters in print is considered more effective at facilitating phoneme–grapheme consolidation than oral phonemic practice in isolation (Ehri et al., 2001). Researchers also advocate explicit teaching of larger phoneme–grapheme units to promote consolidation, as implemented in the current study (Ehri & Snowling, 2006; Hatcher, Hulme, & Ellis, 1994; Wise, Ring, & Olson, 1999).

Related intervention design

Although phonologically-based interventions often produce significant results (Torgesen, 2000), few studies have specifically targeted AA boys who are speakers of NMAE with identified phonological processing deficits or dyslexia. For example, Duff et al. (2014) implemented a reading and language intervention for 171 6-year-old boys and girls with weak reading skills who were at risk for dyslexia as determined by two tests of word reading. The reading strand of the intervention consisted of training in phonological awareness and reading. The language strand focused on training vocabulary and narrative skills through storybooks for themes and structure (Duff et al., 2014). The study revealed that the 9-week intervention was too short to have a significant effect on reading (i.e., foundational) and language (i.e., vocabulary and narrative) skills. The researchers found small to moderate effects of the intervention on foundational skills (i.e., letter knowledge, phoneme awareness, sound deletion) taught through explicit instruction (Duff et al., 2014).

Connor, Thomas-Tate, and Terry (2011) investigated nonmainstream dialect use and literacy acquisition in second-grade students by providing an intervention that included three conditions: business-as-usual control, an editing intervention, and editing with an explicit focus on dialect shifting. This research examined writing samples from speakers of AAE, directing specific attention to AAE morphosyntactic features: plural, past tense, and copula. The intervention with an explicit focus on dialect shifting included an introduction of AAE and AE features, including sentence sorts, feature use practice and editing, and writing and/or editing of the participants' own writing samples. After the intervention, the results suggested that the explicit focus on dialect shifting increased the participants' posttest editing scores.

Researchers (Fogel & Ehri, 2000, 2006) suggest that appropriate approaches to literacy instruction for speakers of AAE consist of explicit instruction, intervention, and the notion of dialect shifting stressing metacognitive flexibility to read and write proficiently. Fogel and Ehri (2000) conducted a study in which they introduced three instructional practices to compare their effectiveness in terms of enhancing AAE speakers' written syntactic competence. The researchers focused on six syntactic features that differ between AAE and school English: possessive *s*, past tense *ed*, third-person present tense singular *s*, plural *s*, indefinite article, and subject–verb agreement. The study concluded that the students who received exposure to text, school English strategies, and guided practice with feedback were more successful on their posttest after the treatment (explicit instruction).

The present study extends a study conducted by the first author that compared differences in reading achievement, knowledge of final consonants and final consonant clusters, phonological awareness skills, and dialect variation among first-grade speakers of NMAE before and after the provision of final consonant phoneme–grapheme mapping through explicit instruction with scaffolding and questions related to a metacognitive understanding of differences between AAE and AE (Russell, 2015). Although the previous study focused on both AA boys and girls, its results revealed that the treatment group exhibited less dialect variation following the intervention than the control group. Also, regression analysis determined that phonological awareness skills contributed to the variance in reading achievement after receptive vocabulary was accounted for. Phonological awareness scores correlated with reading achievement scores. However, there was no difference between the two groups in reading achievement, phonological awareness, or final consonant/cluster encoding and decoding. The study also did not iterate by sex or phonological awareness scores.

The present study

The present study examined differences in reading achievement, phonological awareness skills, and dialect variation between first-grade male speakers of AAE with low phonological awareness (LPA) and average phonological awareness (APA) following a metalinguistic flexibility-based phonological intervention. To do this, we reconfigured data from the first author's previous study (Russell, 2015) through several modifications. First, we analyzed only data from boys in the current study and, in addition, assigned the participants to two groups (i.e., LPA and APA) based on their phonological awareness level as indicated on the CTOPP–2 Elision subtest. Second, we compared differences in pretesting and posttesting between the two phonologically designated groups on reading achievement, phonological awareness, and dialect variation after implementing the intervention for 4 weeks in first-grade classrooms using similar manipulative phonological approaches. Because there were no differences in phonological or reading achievement gains between the control and treatment groups in the original study (Russell, 2015), we did not configure participant groups by those conditions in the current analysis. Finally, while controlling for receptive vocabulary, we analyzed posttest scores for phonological awareness and dialect variation from each group to determine which variable(s) accounted for the variance in reading achievement posttest scores. The following research questions were addressed:

1   When pretest scores are controlled, is there a difference in postintervention reading achievement, phonological awareness skills, and dialect variation between first-grade AA boys with LPA and APA?
2   When receptive vocabulary is controlled, how much variance in reading achievement gains do phonological awareness and dialect variation posttest scores explain?

Method

Participants

The sample consisted of 30 first-grade AA boys enrolled in a Midwestern urban charter school. The average age of the boys in the study was 6.81 years old (LPA group = 7.4 years old, APA group = 6.2 years old). At the time of the study, no participants received special services, and all were eligible for free or reduced lunch. Participants ($n = 17$) who attained a scaled score ($M = 10$, $SD = 3$) of 8 or above on the CTOPP–2 Elision subtest qualified as having APA. Participants ($n = 13$) whose scaled scores on the CTOPP–2 Elision were 7 or lower were placed in the LPA group. Mean scores were 5.77 for the LPA group and 9.24 for the APA group (see Table 1.2). In the LPA group, all participants spoke some or a strong variation of AAE. In the APA group, 16/ 17 participants spoke some or a strong variation of AAE according to the Diagnostic Evaluation of Language Variation–Screener (DELV–S) pretest.

Procedures and measures

The framework for the procedures implemented in this study's design-guided assessment and intervention was based on developing phoneme–grapheme correspondences with a metacognitive understanding of those correspondences. The procedures in this study assumed the ability to associate spoken sound with written letters and understand that associa-tion increases a dialect speaker's ability to decode phonetically and shift from AAE to AE (Thompson, Craig, & Washington, 2004) with meta-linguistic awareness. The study's intervention occurred in daily 30-min whole-group sessions over a 4-week period in spring of the students' first-grade year.

The design for the phoneme–grapheme phonological flexibility-based intervention followed either the procedures from *Phonics and Spelling Through Phoneme-Grapheme Mapping* by Grace (2007) or a phonological manipulation basal series instructional supplement (Shanahan et al., 2013). Words with dialect-sensitive final consonant clusters (e.g., *plan/plant*) were introduced through shared storybook reading and word lists dictated by

Table 1.2 Mean participant age, phonological awareness, dialect variation, and receptive vocabulary scores.

Variable	Achievement measure	LPA (n = 13)	APA (n = 17)
Age		7.4	6.2
Phonological awareness	CTOPP-2 Elision[a]	5.77	9.24
Dialect variation	DELV-S[b]	68.70	62.35
Receptive vocabulary	PPVT-4[c]	82.77	89.29

Note: LPA = low phonological awareness; APA = average phonological awareness; CTOPP-2 = Comprehensive Test of Phonological Processing-Second Edition; DELV-S = Diagnostic Evalua-tion of Language Variation-Screener; PPVT-4 = Peabody Picture Vocabulary Test-Fourth Edition.

a Scaled scores: $M = 10$, $SD = 3$.

b Dialect variation scores were calculated based on the formula by Terry, Connor, Thomas-Tate, and Love (2010). Dialect variation scores represent the percentage of dialect density markers in the total raw score points.

c Standard scores: $M = 100$, $SD = 15$.

the teacher and, in subsequent steps, segmented and blended with blank tiles, decoded, and encoded with simultaneous tile manipulation. The interventions also included a metacognitive aspect, in which both of us used language explicitly modeling phoneme–grapheme manipulation. The first author individually administered and scored the battery of encoding and decoding, phonological awareness, and dialect variation measures listed below prior to and following the 4-week intervention described above. Each assessment's scoring method and data analysis procedures are incorporated into the Results section.

Phonological Awareness Literacy Screening (PALS)

The PALS (Invernizzi, Juel, & Meier, 2007) is a norm-referenced assessment designed for students in prekindergarten through third grade that measures research-suggested emergent literacy factors that may predict reading achievement in later grades. The PALS Word List and Oral Reading in Context subtests were used in this study to measure reading achievement; students silently read a list of single words and orally read a leveled reading passage, respectively, on the two subtests. Reading levels on the Oral Reading in Context subtest were converted to expanded levels for calculation purposes (see Table 1.3).

Researcher-designed (RD) decoding and encoding assessments

These assessments were administered to determine the effectiveness of the intervention at increasing the students' ability to discriminate and manipulate the phonemes in final consonants and final consonant clusters in both decoding and encoding tasks from pretest to posttest. The words on this assessment had final consonants or final consonant clusters with dialect-sensitive features of AAE that were similar spelling patterns to those taught during the intervention. One variable under investigation was the structural features of AAE and the discrepancies with AE, which may contribute to the low reading performance of AA students. Therefore, this tool was developed to investigate the phonological features of AAE, which include the omission of final consonants and reduction of final consonant clusters (Charity et al., 2004).

Devoicing of final consonants, substitution of voiceless consonants for voiced consonants following the vowel (e.g., /his/ for /hiz/), and consonant cluster reduction or the deletion of phonemes from consonant clusters (e.g., the /d/ in *world*) are phonological features of AAE (Craig et al., 2003; Thomas-Tate et al., 2004). Several researchers have investigated final

Table 1.3 Expanded grade level to instructional grade level conversions.

Expanded level	Instructional level
0.0	PP Fr
0.5	PP Ins
1.0	PP Ind
1.5	P Fr
2.0	P Ins
2.5	P Ind
3.0	1 Fr
3.5	1 Ins
4.0	1 Ind
4.5	2 Fr
5.0	2 Ins
5.5	2 Ind
6.0	3 Fr
6.5	3 Ins
7.0	3 Ind

Note: PP = preprimer; Fr = frustration; Ins = instructional; Ind = independent; P = primer.

consonant and final consonant cluster deletion in speakers of AAE (Haynes & Moran, 1989; Seymour & Seymour, 1981; Stockman, 2006; Treiman, 1994). For each RD assessment, students were given 20 words containing common dialectic markers as final consonants or consonant clusters to decode orally or encode in print. The RD assessment also included questions that assessed the metacognitive flexibility thought process, which involved the participant being able to vary his or her encoding (spelling) and decoding (reading) abilities depending on the function or type of task or activity (Cartwright, 2008).

The first author established content validity by reviewing the works of other researchers who have investigated final consonant and final consonant cluster deletion in the speech patterns of AAE speakers (Kligman & Cronnell, 1974; Kohler et al., 2007; Stockman, 2006; Terry, 2006; Terry & Connor, 2010). Items measuring knowledge of final consonant and consonant clusters for the RD assessment were selected from those items cited as having the highest reliability by the aforementioned researchers. In order to ensure interrater reliability, we received a second opinion (from a speaker of AAE and AE) on the selection of words used on the RD assessment. A colleague and a faculty advisor were able to agree that the target words contained dialectally sensitive features of AAE. Also, another colleague (a teacher from the control group) was asked to review the data collection matrix and metacognitive questions and answers to see whether the responses of the participants matched his observations during the intervention.

CTOPP–2 Elision

The CTOPP–2 (Wagner et al., 2013) is a norm-referenced assessment of reading-related phonological processing skills, including phonological awareness, phonological memory, and rapid naming. The CTOPP–2 is written for 5-to 24-year-olds. The Elision subtest used in this research assesses a student's ability to manipulate sound units in words by orally segmenting, deleting, and blending phonemes in a single word.

DELV–S

The DELV–S (Seymour, Roeper, & de Villiers, 2003) is a criterion-referenced assessment screener with two sections designed to measure the extent of language variation from Mainstream American English and risk for language disorder in children ages 4 to 12 years old. This study incorporated only items from the dialect variation section, which assessed both morphosyntactic and phonological features. Students were asked to respond to 15 items: They were presented with pictures of actions, completed cloze statements, answered questions, and were asked to repeat verbatim statements. Response choices included samples characteristic of AE, NMAE, or language disorders.

Peabody Picture Vocabulary Test–Fourth Edition (PPVT–4)

The PPVT–4 (Dunn & Dunn, 2007) is a norm-referenced assessment that measures the receptive vocabulary of children and adults of all abilities. When administering the PPVT–4, the examiner dictates a single word orally and the examinee selects one of four pictures that most closely represents the stimulus word.

Results

This section reports the descriptive statistics, which compare pretest and posttest scaled and raw scores for groups with LPA and APA, and analyses of the data, which compared outcomes of the two groups on all assessments and the prediction of reading achievement by phonological awareness and dialect variation scores. We computed means and standard deviations for pretest measures and then performed an initial data inspection. The inspection revealed that pretest and posttest scores for reading achievement differed between the groups with LPA and APA. For example, mean percentages correct for RD decoding at pretest and posttest were 37.5% and 47.9% for the group with LPA and 81.8% and 85.8% for the group with APA. Similarly, pretest and posttest scores for RD encoding were 18.3% and 27.5% and 61.4% and 68.6%, respectively, for the participant groups with LPA and APA. Table 1.4 provides a summary of the participants' performance on each of the pretest and posttest measures.

Table 1.4 Descriptive statistics for study measures.

Variable	Achievement measure	Phonological deficit				No phonological deficit			
		Pretest		Posttest		Pretest		Posttest	
		M	SD	M	SD	M	SD	M	SD
Reading achievement	PALS Word List[a]	1.73	1.92	2.46	2.41	4.94	2.47	5.59	2.11
	PALS Oral Reading in Context score[a]	1.31	1.51	1.81	1.82	3.82	3.82	4.21	2.29
	RD decoding[b]	37.50	33.24	47.89	37.96	81.77	22.09	85.84	20.65
	RD encoding[b]	18.27	12.76	27.50	24.28	61.38	28.53	68.64	25.80
Phonological awareness	CTOPP-2 Elision[c]	5.77	1.24	6.23	1.59	9.24	1.15	9.59	1.91
Dialect variation	DELV-S	68.70	20.79	68.71	18.94	62.35	17.15	57.23	19.30
Receptive vocabulary	PPVT-4[d]	82.77	8.96	83.54	9.04	89.29	5.78	90.41	5.15

Note: Dialect variation scores were calculated based on the formula by Terry et al. (2010). Dialect variation scores represent the percentage of dialect density markers in the total raw score points. PALS = Phonological Awareness Literacy Screening; RD = researcher-designed; CTOPP-2 = Comprehensive Test of Phonological Processing-Second Edition; DELV-S = Diagnostic Evaluation of Language Variation-Screener; PPVT-4 = Peabody Picture Vocabulary Test-Fourth Edition.

a Conversion table for extended grade level scores (see Table 1.3).
b RD scores are percentages based on raw score correct/total items.
c Scaled scores: $M = 10$, $SD = 3$.
d Standard scores: $M = 100$, $SD = 15$.
a Expanded grade level to instructional grade level conversions.

Comparing group performance following the intervention

We analyzed data using multivariate analysis of variance and multivariate analysis of covariance, controlling for pretest scores, to assess whether there were differences in postintervention reading achievement, phonological awareness skills, and dialect variation for first-grade boys who spoke NMAE with LPA and APA. First we examined the difference in reading achievement between boys with LPA and APA, controlling for pretest scores. Multivariate analysis of covariance was used to analyze the difference in posttest PALS Word List scores and posttest PALS Oral Reading in Context scores, which were used as dependent variables in the model. Multivariate analysis was performed to examine the effect of phonological processing abilities on reading achievement.

After controlling for pretest scores, we found no statistically significant differences in PALS Word List, PALS Oral Reading, RD encoding, or RD decoding scores between boys with LPA and boys with APA, $F(4, 21) = 1.66$, $p = .19$. Therefore, there was no evidence of a difference in posttest reading achievement scores between boys with LPA and APA (see Table 1.5).

We also examined whether, when we controlled for pretest scores, there was a difference in postintervention phonological awareness skills as measured by CTOPP–2 Elision scores. Univariate analysis of covariance was used for this analysis. Controlling for pretest scores, we found no statistically significant differences in phonological awareness between boys with LPA and those with APA, $F(1, 27) = 2.94$, $p = .09$. Therefore, there was no evidence of a difference in phonological awareness between boys with LPA and boys with APA (see Table 1.6).

Table 1.5 Results of a multivariate analysis of covariance to determine differences in PALS Word List, PALS Oral Reading, RD encoding, and RD decoding scores between students with LPA and students with APA.

Source	df	F	p	η_p^2
Intercept	4	1.58	.22	.23
Pretest Word List	4	6.77	.001	.56
Pretest reading passage	4	5.36	.004	.51
Pretest RD encoding	4	1.31	.29	.20
Pretest RD decoding	4	5.73	.004	.52
LPA/APA status	4	1.66	.197	.24

Note: PALS = Phonological Awareness Literacy Screening; RD = researcher-designed; LPA = low phonological awareness; APA = average phonological awareness.

Table 1.6 Results of an analysis of covariance to determine differences in phonological awareness between boys with LPA and boys with APA.

Source	df	F	p	η_p^2
Intercept	1	2.17	.075	.08
Pretest CTOPP Elision	1	3.43	.07	.11
LPA/APA status	1	2.94	.098	.09
Error	27			
Total	30			

Note: LPA = low phonological awareness; APA = average phonological awareness; CTOPP = Comprehensive Test of Phonological Processing.

Table 1.7 Results of an analysis of covariance to determine differences in dialect variation between students with LPA and APA.

Source	df	F	P	η_p^2
Intercept	1	0.074	.79	.003
Pretest DELV-S	1	154.36	<.001	.85
LPA/APA status	1	3.82	.061	.12
Error	27			
Total	30			

Note: LPA = low phonological awareness; APA = average phonological awareness; DELV-S = Diagnostic Evaluation of Language Variation-Screener.

We also examined whether, when we controlled for pretest scores, there was a difference in postintervention dialect variation as measured by posttest dialect variation scores (see Table 1.7). Univariate analysis of covariance was used to analyze this research question. Controlling for pretest scores, we found no statistically significant differences in dialect variation between boys with LPA and boys with APA, $F(1, 27) = 3.82, p = .13$. Therefore, there was no evidence of a difference in dialect variation between boys with LPA and boys with APA (see Table 1.7).

Predicting reading achievement by phonological awareness and dialect variation

We inquired whether, when we controlled for receptive vocabulary knowledge, phonological awareness and dialect variation posttest scores would predict reading achievement posttest scores. Reading achievement posttest scores, dialect variation posttest scores, and phonological awareness posttest scores were analyzed for all students regardless of group to determine whether these relationships held.

When we controlled for receptive vocabulary knowledge, higher CTOPP–2 Elision scores were associated with higher PALS Word List scores, higher PALS Oral Reading scores, higher RD encoding scores, and higher RD decoding scores: PALS Word List, $\beta = 0.73$, $t(27) = 5.01$, $p < .001$; PALS Oral Reading, $\beta = 0.64$, $t(27) = 4.59$, $p < .001$; RD encoding, $\beta = 9.04$, $t(48) = 5.35$, $p < .001$; RD decoding, $\beta = 7.58$, $t(27) = 3.40$, $p = .002$ (see Table 1.8).

Likewise, when controlled for receptive vocabulary knowledge, CTOPP–2 Elision (phonological awareness) scores predicted PALS Word List scores, PALS Oral Reading scores, RD encoding scores, and RD decoding scores in the following sequence: PALS Word List, ΔR^2 .37, $F(1, 27) = 25.06$, $p < .001$; PALS Oral Reading, $\Delta R^2 = .48$, $F(1, 27) = 21.10$, $p < .001$; RD encoding, $\Delta R^2 = .41$, $F(1, 27) = 28.64$, $p < .001$; RD decoding, $\Delta R^2 = .25$, $F(1, 27) = 11.57$, $p = .002$. There was statistically significant evidence that when we controlled for receptive vocabulary knowledge, phonological awareness posttest scores accounted for a significant percentage of the variance in reading achievement posttest scores.

Table 1.8 Results of a hierarchical regression with posttest reading achievement variables as dependent variables and CTOPP-2 Elision as the independent variable.

Dependent variable	PALS Word List		PALS Oral Reading		RD encoding		RD decoding	
	Model 1 (β)	Model 2 (β)	Model 1 (β)	Model 2 (β)	Model 1 (β)	Model 2 (β)	Model 1 (β)	Model 2 (β)
Posttest PPVT-4	0.16**	0.08	0.12*	0.05	1.85*	0.91	1.77*	0.98
Posttest CTOPP-2 Elision		0.73***		0.64***		9.04***		7.58***
ΔR^2	0.21**	0.38***	0.15*	0.37***	0.17*	0.58***	0.16*	0.25***

Note: CTOPP-2 = Comprehensive Test of Phonological Processing-Second Edition; PALS = Phonological Awareness Literacy Screening; RD = researcher-designed; PPVT-4 = Peabody Picture Vocabulary Test-Fourth Edition.

*$p<.05$. **$p<.01$. ***$p<.001$.

Table 1.9 Results of a hierarchical regression with posttest reading achievement variables as dependent variables and dialect variation as the independent variable.

Dependent variable	PALS Word List		PALS Oral Reading		RD encoding		RD decoding	
	Model 1 (β)	Model 2 (β)	Model 1 (β)	Model 2 (β)	Model 1 (β)	Model 2 (β)	Model 1 (β)	Model 2 (β)
Posttest PPVT-4	0.16*	0.10	0.12*	0.07	1.85*	0.99	1.77*	1.26
Posttest dialect variation		−0.06**		−0.06**		−0.92**		−0.54
ΔR²	0.21	0.19	0.15*	0.19*	0.20*	0.27**	0.16*	0.08

Note: PALS = Phonological Awareness Literacy Screening; RD = researcher-designed; PPVT-4 = Peabody Picture Vocabulary Test-Fourth Edition.

$*p < .05. **p < .01.$

In addition, we inquired whether, when we controlled for receptive vocabulary knowledge, dialect variation posttest scores would predict reading achievement posttest scores. Reading achievement posttest scores, dialect variation posttest scores, and phonological awareness posttest scores were analyzed for all students regardless of group to determine if these relationships held.

When we controlled for receptive vocabulary knowledge, lower dialect variation scores were associated with lower PALS Word List scores, lower PALS Oral Reading scores, and lower RD encoding scores as follows: PALS Word List, $\beta = -.064$, $t(27) = -2.91$, $p = .007$; PALS Oral Reading, $\beta = -.57$, $t(27) = -2.79$, $p = .01$; RD encoding, $\beta = 9.04$, $t(48) = 5.35$, $p < .001$.

However, there was no relationship between dialect variation scores and RD decoding scores, $\beta = -.53$, $t(27) = -1.71$, $p = .099$ (see Table 1.9).

In a parallel fashion, when we controlled for receptive vocabulary knowledge, dialect variation scores predicted PALS Word List scores, PALS Oral Reading scores, and RD encoding scores: PALS Word List, $\Delta R^2 = .19$, $F(1, 27) = 8.64$, $p = .007$; PALS Oral Reading, $\Delta R^2 = .19$, $F(1, 27) = 21.10$, $p = .01$; RD encoding, $\Delta R^2 = .27$, $F(1, 27) = 13.66$, $p = .001$.

There was statistically significant evidence that, when we controlled for receptive vocabulary knowledge, dialect variation accounted for a significant percentage of the variance in PALS Word List scores, PALS Oral Reading scores, and RD encoding posttest scores. However, there was no evidence that dialect variation accounted for a significant percentage of the variance in RD decoding scores.

Discussion

The present study extends the research conducted in the Russell (2015) study, in which both male and female first-grade speakers of AAE participated in a metalinguistic phonologically based intervention. However, the present study examined data only from AA boys who were assigned to two phonologically designated groups based on their CTOPP–2 Elision subtest scores. We wanted to examine differences in postintervention reading achievement, phonological awareness skills, and dialect variation between the two groups of first-grade AA boys when we controlled for pretest scores. Results of the statistical analysis indicated that the pretest and posttest differences between the two groups were not significant; thus, the intervention was equally effective for both groups.

Although we found no statistically significant differences between the two groups in posttest reading achievement scores, phonological awareness scores, or dialect variation scores when we controlled for pretests, inspection revealed differing raw data. Both RD measures indicated higher mean percentage correct gains for the group with LPA as well as pretest-level correspondence to the groups' LPA/APA status. On the RD decoding assessment, the LPA mean percentage correct increased from 37.5% to 47.9%, whereas the corresponding APA mean percentage increased from 81.8% to 85.8%. Similarly, the LPA encoding mean percentage correct increased from 18.3% to 27.5%, whereas the APA encoding mean percentage correct moved from 61.4% to 68.6%. These informal results based on inspection would seem to suggest that the phonologically based intervention improved decoding and encoding mean raw scores for the group with LPA.

Notwithstanding these results, we also describe a group of three students in the group with LPA whose raw scores on all reading achievement assessments were 0 at pretest and posttest. On the CTOPP–2 Elision subtest, the three students had scaled scores of 3, 5, and 5, all below the LPA group mean of 5.8. Although the variance in this group's scores from the remainder of the LPA achievement scores may have contributed to the broad standard deviations for the LPA group, data from these three students may also indicate that the 4-week whole-group intervention was not effective for some students with greater need. Students at this pretest level may require an intensity of intervention provided through longer and individualized instruction. Congruent with this, Snowling and Hulme (2011) examined evidence-based interventions for reading and language difficulties (i.e., dyslexia, which they defined as a specific reading disorder) and concluded that some students with a decoding difficulty caused by phonological processing may require an "individualized approach that is ongoing and many need to continue through the school years" (Snowling & Hulme, 2011, p. 19).

We also investigated how much variance in reading achievement gains phonological awareness and dialect variation posttest scores accounted for in each group when we controlled for receptive vocabulary scores. Controlling for receptive vocabulary adjusts for the students who have higher vocabulary knowledge according to the PPVT–4. Students' vocabulary knowledge is a predictor of reading achievement, and those students who have higher vocabulary knowledge generally outperform lower students in reading achievement (Scarborough, 2001). The results revealed that higher phonological awareness posttest scores were associated with reading achievement posttest scores (see Table 1.8). These findings suggest that increasing students' phonological abilities increases reading achievement for students with both LPA and APA and additionally support findings from other studies that state that phonological awareness skills predict reading ability (Nancollis, Lawrie, & Dodd, 2005; Schuele & Boudreau, 2008).

Also, dialect variation scores were associated with all reading achievement measures except for RD decoding scores (see Table 1.9). It is possible that the participants could increasingly negotiate the differences between AAE and AE because of the metalinguistic component integrated with literacy acquisition in the classroom culture throughout the school year. The findings are consistent with a study conducted by Terry and Connor (2010), who examined the linguistic flexibility of NMAE-speaking children in kindergarten through the end of first grade. These researchers concluded that children increased their production of AE by the end of the school year as a result of the growing linguistic and orthographic ability that comes with learning how to read. In all, our findings indicate that pretest to posttest reading achievement measures were similar for both groups and that both phonological awareness and dialect variation predicted reading achievement. It is also likely that a longer individually administered phonological intervention focused on the specific instructional needs of AA boys with LPA may be necessary for some students.

Implications for practice and future research

The present study examined the roles of phonological awareness and dialect variation in response to a metacognitive phonological awareness–based intervention for first-grade AA boys. However, a few limitations should be addressed. The sample size consisted of only 30 AA boys from one urban charter school; results cannot be generalized from this limited representation of AA boys. There is also a need for qualitative research in this study that would provide more detailed description of the variables, student verbal metalinguistic response, and the observable gains made by the students in written and oral samples. The data from a subgroup of three boys in the LPA group who scored 0 on all reading achievement pretests and most posttests may have confounded both the degree of variance in the LPA standard deviations and the accuracy of the differences from pretest to posttest between the two groups. Data from the subgroup of three boys were included in the data collection because their removal would not have changed the results pertinent to the specific research questions analyzed and discussed in this study. The subgroup may not have mastered previously taught phonemic decoding skills and consequently was not ready to progress to final consonant mapping in a whole-group setting.

In response to these limitations, future research is needed with a larger and more representative sample of AA boys. Future studies should also investigate the effects of varying durations and intensities of interventions on metacognitive phoneme–grapheme correspondence on reading acquisition, particularly for AA boys who struggle with phonological awareness tasks. Also, additional statistical processing of the data from Russell's (2015) study, which included the creation of a third subgroup and further analysis of progress from pretest to posttest, would provide additional information on the intervention's effectiveness for students with a range of phonological ability levels.

Despite the stated limitations, the findings of the present study have implications for practice. Because both phonological awareness ability and dialect variation accounted for variance in the reading achievement of AA boys with both LPA and APA, an increased emphasis on related instructional components may be promising. When designing assessment and instruction for AA boys, it appears important to consider the role these factors may play in students' progress. Educators should make instructional decisions based on the phonological awareness abilities of students who are at risk for reading difficulties. Early identification of phonological deficits and timely intense intervention of adequate duration are critical for future literacy proficiency (Torgesen, 2000). The metalinguistic flexibility component included in this intervention focused on providing explicit instruction incorporating phonemic manipulation and verbal scaffolding related to a metacognitive understanding of phonological differences between AAE and AE.

In classroom or small-group settings, teachers can implement similar modeling and linguistic scaffolds targeting both the phonological awareness abilities and dialectic differences of AA boys. To facilitate a classroom culture of respect for many AA boys' home language and empower AAE/AE exchange self-efficacy, educators must also expand their knowledge base on the systematic nature of AAE and effective dialect-shifting strategies (e.g., see Wheeler and Swords, 2006). In conclusion, results from the present study suggest that best practices for promoting the literacy proficiency of AA boys encompass implementing adequately intense and timely intervention adjusted for a wide range of phonological abilities in a culturally responsive linguistic context.

References

Bacon, E., Banks, J., Young, K., & Jackson, F. (2007). Perceptions of African American and European American teachers on the education of African American boys. *Multiple Voices, 10*(1&2), 160–172.

Baker, C., Cameron, C., Rimm-Kaufman, S., & Grissmer, D. (2012). Family and sociodemographic predictors of school readiness among African American boys in kindergarten. *Early Education and Development, 23*, 833–854.

Blomert, L., & Willems, G. (2010). Is there a causal link from a phonological awareness deficit to reading failure in children at familial risk for dyslexia? *Wiley Online Library, 16*(4), 300–317. DOI: 10.1002/dys.405.

Cartwright, K. B. (Ed.). (2008). *Literacy processes: Cognitive flexibility in learning and teaching.* New York, NY: Guilford.

Charity, A. H., Scarborough, H. S., & Griffin, D. M. (2004). Familiarity with School English in African American children and its relation to early reading achievement. *Child Development, 75*, 1340–1356.

Connor, C. M., Thomas-Tate, T., & Terry, N. P. (July (2011). Society for the Scientific Study of Reading, St. Augustine, FL.

Craig, H. K., Thompson, C., Washington, J. A., & Potter, S. (2003). Performance of elementary-grade African American students on the gray oral reading tests. *Language, Speech, and Hearing Services in Schools, 35*, 141–154.

Craig, H. K., Zhang, L., Hensel, S., & Quinn, E. (2009). African American English-speaking students: An examination of relationship between dialect shifting and reading outcomes. *Journal of Speech, Language, and Hearing Research, 52*, 839–855.

Duff, F. J., Hume, C., Grainger, K., Hardwick, S. J., Miles, J., N., & Snowing, M. (2014). Reading and language intervention for children at risk of dyslexia: A randomized controlled trail. *Journal of Child Psychology and Psychiatry, 55*(11), 1234–1243.

Dunn, L., & Dunn, D. (2007). *Peabody Picture Vocabulary Test* (4th ed.). Bloomington, MN: NCS Pearson, Inc. Educational Testing Service. (2011). Addressing achievement gaps: Positioning young Black boys for educational success. *Policy Notes, 19*(3), 1–15. Retrieved from https://www.ets.org/Media/Research/pdf/PIC-PNV19n3.pdf

Ehri, L. C. (1997). Learning to read and learning to spell are one and the same, almost. In C. A. Perfecta, L. Rueben, & M. Fayol (Eds.), *Learning to spell: Research, theory, and practice across languages* (pp. 237–269). Mahwah, NJ: Erlbaum.

Ehri, L., Nunes, S., Willows, D., Schuster, B., Yaghoub-Zadeh, Z., & Shanahan, T. (2001). Phonemic awareness instruction helps children learn to read: Evidence from the National Reading Panel's meta-analysis. *Reading Research Quarterly*, 36, 250–287.

Ehri, L. C., & Snowling, M. J. (2006). Developmental variation in word recognition. In C. A. Stone, E. R. Silliman,B. J. Ehren, & K. Apel (Eds.), *Handbook of language and literacy: Development and disorders* (pp. 433–460). New York: NY: The Guilford Press.

Fogel, H., & Ehri, C. L. (2000). Teaching elementary students who speak Black English vernacular to write in Standard English: Effects of dialect transformation practice. *Contemporary Educational Psychology*, 25, 212–235.

Fogel, H., & Ehri, L. (2006). Teaching African American English forms to Standard American English-speaking teachers: Effects on acquisition, attitudes, and responses to student use. *Journal of Teacher Education*, 57, 464–480.

Grace, K. (2007). *Phonics and spelling through phoneme-grapheme mapping*. Boston, MA: Sopris West Educational Services.

Hatcher, P., J., Hulme, C., & Ellis, A. W. (1994). Ameliorating early reading failure by integrating the teaching of reading and phonological skills: The phonological linkage hypothesis. *Child Development*, 65, 41–57.

Haynes, W., & Moran, M. (1989). A cross-sectional developmental study of final consonant production in southern Black children from preschool through third grade. *Language, Speech, and Hearing Services in Schools*, 20, 400–406.

Invernizzi, M., Juel, C., & Meier, J. (2007). Phonological Awareness Literacy Screening. University of Virginia. Curry School of Education.

Joe, E., & Davis, J. E. (2009). Parental influence, school readiness, and early academic achievement of African American boys. *The Journal of Negro Education*, 78(3), 260–276.

Joly-Pottuz, B., Mercier, M., Leynaud, A., & Habib, M. (2008). Combined auditory and articulatory training improves phonological deficit in children with dyslexia. *Neuropsychological Rehabilitation*, 18(4), 402–429.

Juel, C., Griffith, P. L., & Gough, P. B. (1986). Acquisition of literacy: A longitudinal study of children in first and second grade. *Journal of Educational Psychology*, 78, 243–255.

Kligman, D. S., & Cronnell, B. A. (1974). Black English and spelling. Southwest Regional Laboratory for Educational Research and Development Technical Report No. 50. Washington, DC: US Department of Health, Education and Welfare. (ERIC Document Reproduction Service ED 108 234).

Kohler, C. T., Bahr, R. H., Silliman, E. R., Bryant, J. B., Apel, K., & Wilkinson, L. C. (2007). African American English dialect and performance on nonword spelling and phonemic awareness tasks. *American Journal of Speech-Language Pathology*, 16, 157–168.

Ladson-Billings, G. (2006). From the achievement gap to the education debt: Understanding achievement in U. S. schools. *Educational Research*, 35(7), 3–12.

Lee, C. (2005). Culture and language: Bidialectical issues in literacy. In J. Flood & P. Anders (Eds.), *Literacy development of students in urban schools: Research and policy* (pp. 241–274). Newark, DE: The International Reading Association.

Lyon, G. R., Shaywitz, S. E., & Shaywitz, B. A. (2003). Defining dyslexia, comorbidity, Teachers' knowledge of language and reading: A definition of dyslexia. *Annals of Dyslexia*, 53, 1–14.

Mangino, W. (2009). The downside of social closure: Brokerage, parental influence, and delinquency amongAfrican American boys. *Sociology of Education*, 82, 147–172.

McWayne, C. M., Owsianik, M., Green, L. E., & Fantuzzo, J. W. (2008). Parenting behaviors and preschool children's social and emotional skills: A question of the consequential validity of traditional parenting constructs for low-income African Americans. *Early Childhood Research Quarterly*, 23(2), 173–192.

Moran, M. (1993). Final consonant deletion in African American children speaking Black English: A closer look. *Language, Speech, and Hearing Services in Schools*, 24, 161–166.

Nancollis, A., Lawrie, B., & Dodd, B. (2005). Phonological intervention and the acquisition of literacy skills in children from deprived social backgrounds. *Language, Speech, and Hearing Services in Schools*, 36(4), 325–335.

Odegard, T. N., Ring, J., Smith, S., Biggan, J., & Black, J. (2008). Differentiating the neural response to intervention in children with developmental dyslexia. *The International Dyslexia Association*, 58(1), 1–14. Published Online 16 May 2008.

Parker, F., & Riley, K. (2005). *Linguistics for non-linguists: A primer with exercises.* Boston: Allyn & Bacon.

Richards, E. (2016). Wisconsin no.1 for black-white science achievement gap. *The Milwaukee Journal Sentinel.* Retrieved from http://www.jsonline.com

Rickford, J. R., & Rickford, R. J. (2000). *Spoken soul: The story of Black English.* New York, NY: Wiley.

Russell, J. G. (2015). The influence of a metalinguistic flexibility-based phonological intervention on the language and literacy skills of first grade speakers of nonmainstream American English (Doctoral dissertation). Retrieved from http://www.stritch.edu/library.

Scarborough, H. S (2001). Connecting early language and literacy to later reading (dis)abilities: Evidence, theory, and practice. In S. B. Neuman, & D. K. Dickinson (Eds.), *Handbook of early literacy research* (pp. 97–110). New York: Guilford Press.

Schuele, C., & Boudreau, D. (2008). Phonological awareness intervention: Beyond the basics. *Language, Speech, and Hearing Services in Schools*, 39(1), 3–20.

Seymour, H., Roeper, T., & de Villiers, J. (2003). *Diagnostic evaluation of language variation-screening test.* San Antonio, TX: Harcourt Assessment, Inc.

Seymour, H., & Seymour, C. (1981). Black English and Standard American English contrasts in consonantal development of four-and five-year-old children. *Journal of Speech and Hearing Disorders*, 46, 274–280.

Shanahan, T., Fisher, D., Kilgo, M., Hasbrouck, J., Gibson, V., Echevarria, J. . . . Zike, D. (2013). *Reading wonders.* New York, NY: McGraw-Hill.

Snowling, M, & Hulme, C. (2011). Evidence-based interventions for reading and language difficulties: Creating a virtuous circle. *British Journal of Educational Psychology*, 81, 1–23.

Stanovich, K. E. (1988). The right and wrong places to look for the cognitive locus of reading disability. *Annals of Dyslexia, 38,* 154–177.

Stockman, I. (2006). Alveolar bias in the final consonant deletion patterns of African American children. *Language, Speech, and Hearing Services in Schools, 37,* 85–95.

Terry, N. P. (2006). Relations between dialect variation, grammar, and early spelling skills. *Reading and Writing, 19,* 907–931.

Terry, N. P., & Connor, C. (2010). African American English and spelling: How do second graders spell dialect-sensitive feature of words? *Learning Disability Quarterly, 33,* 199–210.

Terry, N. P., Connor, C., Petscher, Y., & Conlin, C. (2012). Dialect variation and reading: Is change in nonmainstream American English use related to reading achievement in first and second grade? *Journal of Speech, Language, and Hearing Research, 55,* 55–69.

Terry, N. P., Connor, C., Thomas-Tate, S., & Love, M. (2010). Examining relationships among dialect variation, literacy skills, and school context in first grade. *Journal of Speech, Language, and Hearing Research, 53,* 126–145.

Thomas-Tate, S., Washington, J., & Edwards, J. (2004). Standardized assessment of phonological awareness skills in low-income African American first graders. *American Journal of Speech-Language Pathology, 13,* 182–190.

Thompson, C. A., Craig, H. K., & Washington, J. A. (2004). Variable production of African American English across oracy and literacy contexts. *Language, Speech, and Hearing Services in Schools, 35,* 269–282.

Torgesen, J. K. (2000). Individual differences in response to early interventions in reading: The lingering problem of treatment resisters. *Learning Disabilities Research & Practice, 15,* 55–64.

Treiman, R. (1994). Use of consonant letter names in beginning spelling. *Developmental Psychology, 30,* 567–580.

Wagner, R., Torgesen, J., Rashotte, C., & Pearson, D. (2013). *Comprehensive test of phonological processing* (2nd ed.). Austin, TX: PRO-ED.

Washington, J. A., & Craig, H. K. (1994). Dialectal forms during discourse of poor, urban, African-American preschoolers. *Journal of Speech and Hearing Research, 37,* 816–823.

Wheeler, R., & Swords, R. (2006). *Code-switching: Teaching standard English in urban classrooms.* Urbana: National Council of Teachers of English.

Wisconsin Department of Public Instruction. (January 13, 2016). *State results issued for Badger Exam.* Retrieved from http://www.dpi.wi.gov.

Wise, B. W., Ring, J., & Olson, R. K. (1999). Training phonological awareness with and without explicit attention to articulation. *Journal of Experimental Child Psychology, 72,* 271–304.

2 Reading and language performance of low-income, African American boys in Grades 1–5

Julie A. Washington, Lee Branum-Martin, Ryan Lee-James, and Congying Sun

Individual differences in the performance of young children can be influenced by a host of sociodemographic and environmental factors, including socioeconomic status (SES), race, culture, gender, age, and quality of the home and school environments. These factors frequently interact to influence various child outcomes. The role of gender in the performance of boys compared to girls has been examined across several skill areas with mixed results. In the case of language and reading, it has been widely reported that girls develop a range of linguistic skills at an accelerated rate and at younger ages than do boys (Bauer, Goldfield, & Reznick, 2002; Eriksson et al., 2012; Huttenlocher, Haight, Bryk, Seltzer, & Lyons, 1991; Hyde & Linn, 1988; Maccoby & Jacklin, 1974) and that they also outpace their male peers in the development of early reading skills (Caro, McDonald, & Willms, 2009; Flannery, Liederman, Daly, & Schultz, 2000; Liederman, Kantrowitz, & Flannery, 2005; Logan & Johnston, 2010; McGeown, Goodwin, Henderson, & Wright, 2012). Despite seemingly strong and well-accepted evidence of the presence of gender differences, many empirical studies challenge these findings, showing either no gender differences for boys compared to girls in these important skill areas (Shaywitz, Shaywitz, Fletcher, & Escobar, 1990) or reporting strengths for boys over girls (Kidd & Lum, 2008; Logan & Johnston, 2010).

Gender differences in the development of reading and language skills have also been reported by race. In particular, African American boys are reportedly at highest risk for the development of poor outcomes in these and other achievement areas. Utilizing data from the National Assessment of Educational Progress (NAEP), Husband (2012b) and others (Davis, 2003; Jencks & Phillips, 2011) have discussed substantial race gaps in reading performance nationally, with African American boys performing significantly lower than Asian, White, Hispanic, and American Indian boys at fourth grade. In the early years the language and reading gaps between

African American and White boys are reportedly evident as young as toddler age for language and preschool age for reading (Aratani, Wight, & Cooper, 2011). However, when researchers control for influential variables such as SES and child-level variables such as low birth weight and family support, the race gap for Black boys reportedly disappears by kindergarten (Aratani et al., 2011; Iruka, 2017). These findings are in contrast to several studies that report substantial gaps in achievement for African American boys throughout their schooling experience regardless of SES (Fantuzzo, LeBoeuf, Rouse, & Chen, 2012).

Though many studies highlight a gender gap in language and reading in early childhood, the findings are equivocal for school-age children. It is evident that something important happens between kindergarten and 12th grade when the performance of African American students in general and African American boys in particular reportedly diverges sharply from the performance of their peers. There are very few studies focused on this Race × Gender interaction in the achievement of school-age African American boys.

Many of these studies are cross-sectional and vary widely in age and grade ranges examined, sample size, and academic and cognitive skills assessed. In many of these studies, reading is represented as a combined achievement outcome, either as a composite score along with other associated academic skills (e.g., critical thinking, distinguishing real and imaginary text, and the ability to connect text with personal life experiences) without disaggregation of core reading skills (e.g., decoding, fluency, and comprehension; Matthews, Kizzie, Rowley, & Cortina, 2010) or as a criterion-based, pass/fail outcome (i.e., failing in one or more content areas, such as reading, math, or both; Connell, Spencer, & Aber, 1994), which makes it difficult to isolate the effect of gender on reading. The purpose of the current study was to characterize the development of language, reading, and cognition in African American boys in first through fifth grades utilizing a longitudinal, accelerated cohort design in an effort to contribute to understanding of the growth trajectories of these critical skills during elementary grades, a foundational time in schooling.

Gender differences in language

It is a long-held belief that boys develop language at a different rate than girls, with girls being superior to boys in overall verbal development (Anastasi, 1958; Hyde & Linn, 1988; Maccoby & D'Andrade, 1966; Maccoby & Jacklin, 1974). In particular, research in early childhood indicates that boys lag behind girls in their development of vocabulary, gestures, word combining, utterance length, and complexity (Bauer et al., 2002; Eriksson et al., 2012; Huttenlocher et al., 1991). In an investigation of gender-based language differences in infancy and toddlerhood across 10 non-English language communities, Eriksson et al. (2012) demonstrated that beginning as early as infant communication, including gestures, girls were ahead of boys developmentally, though effect sizes were quite small, accounting for <1% of the variance in performance.

Similarly, Bauer et al. (2002) and Huttenlocher et al. (1991) found significant differences in lexical development between boys and girls who were 2 years of age or younger. Though these gender differences are consistently evident in early childhood, by the time children reach school age, the language gap between boys and girls reportedly disappears (Maccoby & D'Andrade, 1966; Maccoby & Jacklin, 1974). It is important to note that because of the young ages of children in these investigations, parent-report measures are most often used to estimate the size of children's vocabulary and the extent of their expressive and receptive language skills. Though this is an appropriate methodology for use with very young children, self-report has widely acknowledged limitations in terms of accurate characterization of gender differences in early language abilities.

Studies of gender differences in school-age children have reported less consistent conclusions, and fewer recent articles are available. In an early meta-analysis of studies focused on gender differences in language ability, Maccoby and Jacklin (1974) concluded that the preponderance of the evidence suggested that the language development rate and skills of boys and girls were very similar from preschool through preadolescence. At approximately 10 or 11 years of age there is a divergence, such that girls outperform boys linguistically, and this advantage continues through high school. According to Maccoby and Jacklin (1974), the magnitude of the gender difference in performance can vary but amounts to approximately 0.25 *SD*.

Most important perhaps is that of 85 studies examined, 70% reported no gender differences at all in verbal abilities, 25% reported an advantage for females, and the remaining 5% reported an advantage for the males in their samples. These studies varied widely in terms of sample sizes, verbal abilities assessed, and the age ranges of participants. In stark contrast, Hyde and Linn (1988) concluded in a later meta-analysis that "the magnitude of the gender difference in verbal ability is currently so small that it can effectively be considered to be zero" (p. 64). These findings were supported in a later epidemiological study focused on the identification of specific language impairment in a diverse sample of kindergartners, which determined that boys are no more likely than girls to be identified as having a specific language impairment (Tomblin et al., 1997), debunking a long-held belief regarding significant differences in impairment rates for boys compared to girls.

Gender differences in reading

Gender differences in the development of important academic skills, including reading, are widely reported (Caro et al., 2009; Flannery et al., 2000; Kingdon, Serbin, & Stack, 2017; Liederman et al., 2005; McGeown et al., 2012; Raag et al., 2011). Similar to language, the gap in reading ability between boys and girls appears to widen with age (Logan & Johnston, 2010). Kingdon et al. (2017) examined the developmental reading trajectories of 126 low-income male and female children from elementary to secondary school and found that all children performed similarly in elementary school but that a gender gap in academic performance emerged in secondary school. That is, girls outperformed boys beginning in secondary school; boys continued to experienced difficulty through secondary school, while girls' performance remained stable.

In a meta-analysis focused on overall grades by gender across academic subject areas, Voyer and Voyer (2014) also found a consistent advantage for females from elementary school through the university level. The advantage was more pronounced for language-based subjects and less pronounced for math. Also similar to the gender advantage identified for language, the gender differences in reading in the Voyer and Voyer analysis evidenced relatively small effect sizes, which has been reported by others (McGeown et al., 2012). In contrast, in a study of low-income boys and girls, Kingdon et al. (2017) reported that both boys' and girls' performance decelerated in secondary school, with boys declining at a faster rate than girls. Furthermore, they found evidence of an advantage for females in both reading and math and estimated that females outperformed males by about 0.25 *SD* across all subject areas. This estimated effect size was reported for language as well (Maccoby & Jacklin, 1974).

It is important to note that many factors have been identified as contributing to the reading achievement gap between boys and girls, including motivation, differential attitudes toward reading, and differences in teacher and parent expectations of boys and girls. Overall, the literature in reading is more consistent than that in language. Whereas gender differences in language are debated, most investigators examining gender and reading agree that there is a difference in performance, with girls having an advantage over boys. The age at which the difference emerges and the magnitude of the difference continue to be discussed.

The language and reading of African American boys

Studies focused on the impact of gender on language and reading for African American children contrast significantly with the literature reported above, which either was not focused on or did not include African

American children in substantial numbers. African American children overall perform poorly in school, and within this racial subgroup of American students, African American boys reportedly perform significantly more poorly than African American girls. Indeed, studies of achievement focused on African American children report large gender disparities beginning in infancy and persisting throughout schooling (Aratani et al., 2011; Flannery et al., 2000; Harris & Graves, 2010; Matthews et al., 2010; Roberts, Burchinal, & Durham, 1999).

Studies of the race and gender gap in education for African American children rely largely on data documenting the Black/White achievement gap reported nationally for fourth, eighth, and 12th graders on the NAEP, also called the *Nation's Report Card* (Bohrnstedt, Kitmitto, Ogut, Sherman, & Chan, 2015). Outcomes of the NAEP have documented a long-standing gap in achievement between African American children and their White and Asian peers in reading, mathematics, and other academic subject areas. When these race gap data are disaggregated further by gender there is a smaller measurable gap in performance between African American boys and both White and African American girls. In the current study, African American girls enrolled in the same schools and living in the same neighborhoods provided a natural comparison group.

Language

As reading is a consistent area of educational concern at the national, state, and local levels, there are many more studies focused on reading than on the general language use and development of African American boys. Studies of the language of African American students tend to focus more on language variation than on general language ability and seldom consider gender. Those language studies that are available compare African American boys either to White boys, describing a gap that is more race than gender based, or to African American girls. In a report focused on the race gap in very young children, Aratani et al. (2011) examined the performance of African American boys compared to White boys in preschool and kindergarten on a number of developmental measures, including language, utilizing a large sample from the Early Childhood Longitudinal Study-Birth Cohort. Across all experimental measures, including language and reading, White boys significantly outperformed African American boys. In the case of reading, African American boys scored 0.10 *SD* to 0.20 *SD* below their White peers in both preschool and kindergarten. The language gap was more significant at these ages and reportedly increased with age. For both reading and language, the race gap disappeared when SES was controlled, which suggests that perhaps the gaps observed are driven by low SES rather than race.

Roberts et al. (1999) examined the language skills of a longitudinal cohort of 87 low-income African American boys and girls at 18, 24, and 30 months of age. They measured vocabulary and grammatical development using both parent reporting and standardized language tests appropriate participants. Results indicated that girls had larger vocabularies, used longer utterances, and used more irregular noun and verb forms than boys. Effect sizes were large for vocabulary differences at 24 months (Cohen's $d = 1.08$) and moderate for grammatical differences (Cohen's $d = 0.63$). The gender differences in grammatical development reported by Roberts et al. for low-income African American boys and girls were also found in an investigation of the narrative performance of older African American children (11–12.5 years; Mainess, Champion, & McCabe, 2012).

With the exception of Mainess et al. (2012), studies focused on the gender gap in language for African American boys mirror those for non-African American children in that they are focused on very young children. In the case of African American boys, however, the gaps in language have larger reported effect sizes, which suggests that African American girls perform significantly better than boys at these young ages regardless of SES. In addition, these outcomes are reportedly influenced by a host of sociodemographic and environmental variables that affect outcomes for boys, including SES, parental education, quality of the home environment, and amount of language input received (Aratani et al., 2011; Roberts et al., 1999; Tamis-LeMonda, Song, Leavell, Kahana-Kalman, & Yoshikawa, 2012).

Reading

Though still few in quantity, there have been several more papers focused on the poor reading achievement of African American boys than on general language skills, though many are not data based. It is important to note that many of these studies do not adequately address both race and gender. That is, the focus is often on the race gap between White and African American boys rather than the gender gap between boys and girls. For example, Fantuzzo et al. (2012) utilized a cumulative risk framework to examine the differences in performance of urban African American and White boys on a range of academic skills, including reading. As has been reported elsewhere, there was a reading gap between African American and White boys, with African American boys performing more poorly on reading assessments as well as on assessments of mathematics. This difference by race is well documented both in the extant literature (Husband, 2012a, 2012b; Matthews et al., 2010) and on the NAEP (Bohrnstedt et al., 2015).

In a longitudinal investigation focused on gender and race differences, Matthews et al. (2010) examined the literacy gap in a large sample of

African American boys and girls and White boys and girls in kindergarten and first, third, and fifth grades from the Early Childhood Longitudinal Study-Kindergarten Cohort 1998–1999. Similar to many other studies, they found both gender and race gaps in the development of literacy in kindergarten between African American boys and their peers. The race gap was more pronounced than the gender gap, producing moderate effect sizes, but both gaps continued to increase in magnitude through fifth grade. These authors noted that the African American boys in the sample were also more likely to be from low-income homes with poor home literacy environments. The additive effects of gender and race were identified as influential in the poor performance of African American boys in the sample.

Utilizing the same kindergarten cohort and first-grade cohort, Chatterji (2006) reported similar outcomes for African American children in the early grades. They confirmed that the reading gaps between boys and girls and between African Americans and Whites continued to grow in size across these early grades and that these outcomes were most pronounced for children from low-income households, which characterized most of the African American boys in the sample.

McMillian, Frierson, and Campbell (2011) focused on the performance of a small ($n = 113$) sample of low-income African American boys and girls at ages 8 and 12, utilizing a secondary data analysis of children who participated in a randomized trial focused on educational intervention. They hypothesized that there would be no differences in mathematics or reading achievement at age 8 but that girls would outperform boys at age 12. However, the hypothesis was not supported, as no gender differences in either reading or mathematics achievement were evident at either age. Unfortunately, the sample size limited this study's statistical power to detect differences in a sample of children who exhibited very little variation in academic performance overall.

Overall, studies focused on the performance of African American boys on reading measures present mixed findings. Whereas many articles present an overwhelming impression that these boys are failing academically compared to their peers regardless of race (Davis, 2003; Husband, 2012a, 2012b), and data-based research supports the consistent presence of race differences in performance, gender differences are less clear. An exception is Justice, Invernizzi, Geller, Sullivan, and Welsch (2005), who found a gender gap between girls and boys but no race gap between African American and White boys in most early literacy skills. Taken together, these investigations suggest that African American boys may or may not perform differently from girls in terms of the development of reading skills. When these differences are present, however, the data suggest that they persist throughout schooling and that income status substantially influences performance.

Individual differences in academic trajectories

The current investigation applied an individual change score model to examine the reading and language trajectories of African American boys compared to girls in first through fifth grades. Though few studies were available in the literature to guide our thinking about language trajectories for African American boys, three distinct types of longitudinal findings have been reported in the literature for children who are at risk for failure as a result of a variety of sociodemographic variables (e.g., differences attributed to SES, school readiness or learning-related skills such as executive function and social skills; Matthews et al., 2010; McClelland, Acock, & Morrison, 2006). The first type of longitudinal finding is stable growth in reading or math achievement over time with no significant increases or decreases in performance across grades (Caro et al., 2009; McClelland et al., 2006; McMillian et al., 2011). The second type of longitudinal finding is a narrowing of performance differences over time between groups by race or gender (Curby, Rimm-Kaufman, & Ponitz, 2009; Iruka, Gardner-Neblett, Matthews, & Winn, 2014). The third type of finding is a widening of achievement gaps between groups over time (Caro et al., 2009; Chatterji, 2006; Curby et al., 2009; Matthews et al., 2010; McClelland et al., 2006).

Evidence from this literature indicates that the type of longitudinal trajectory may vary as a function of a number of variables, including age and grade. For example, Caro et al. (2009) examined math performance from first grade through high school as it related to the SES of participants. Math performance remained stable from second through sixth grades regardless of SES, but the gap between students from lower and higher SES backgrounds widened from seventh through 10th grades. Curby et al. (2009) found that children who demonstrated higher reading ability at the start of kindergarten grew faster than their peers who started out at lower levels, which implies that the gap between these two groups would widen in subsequent grades. Conversely, children who started out with higher performance in math and phonological awareness grew more slowly than their peers who started out lower, which suggests a narrowing of the gap in subsequent grades.

The current study

It is not clear from the evidence in the extant literature which of these three trajectories – stable growth over time, narrowing of performance differences, or widening of performance gaps – characterizes the reading and language growth of African American boys and how the trajectory is different compared to African American girls in the same schools. There have been both studies that report a widening of the gender gap throughout schooling (Aratani et al., 2011; Caro et al., 2009; Matthews et al., 2010; McClelland et al., 2006) and others that suggest that these differences may be resolved during the early years (Iruka et al., 2014). These studies further suggest that the trajectory may be quite different for language versus reading. The current longitudinal study permitted an examination of growth in both reading and language across a large sample of African American boys and girls, all of whom attended the same schools. The performance of males was compared to that of females.

Results in the extant literature do not provide a clear picture of the gender differences in performance that may exist for African American boys. Is there an overarching boy problem, as has been suggested (Davis, 2003; Husband, 2012a, 2012b), such that the performance of African American boys is significantly different from that of girls? If differences are identified, how do they change with increasing age or grade? In order to address these important issues, we posed the following research question: How do African American boys and girls differ in the longitudinal development of reading, cognition, and language in first through fifth grades?

Method

Participants

Participants were enrolled in a larger project focused on language, literacy, and dialectal variation. African American boys and girls ($N = 890$) were investigated in first through fifth grades in a major urban school district in the southeastern United States. Participants ranged in age from 5.8 to 12.5 years of age ($M = 8.3$, $SD = 1.3$ years). Approximately half (48%) of the participants were male and half were female. At the beginning of each academic year, children were recruited for participation during school orientation sessions. Doctoral students and doctoral-level project personnel (e.g., research scientists and project coordinators) were responsible for attending the orientation to disseminate details of the study to families and distribute consent forms.

All children who returned consent forms were considered for inclusion in the current study. Participants attended seven different schools in the public elementary schools – four schools were traditional public schools and the remaining three were public charter schools. Across all seven schools, eligibility for the National School Lunch Program ranged from 50% to 100%, with the highest percentages of children eligible for free and reduced-price lunch attending the traditional public schools.

In the current study, we only included children who were not enrolled in special education services and had complete information on gender.

Accordingly, 55 children receiving special education services and four children with missing information on gender were excluded from the current study, which resulted in a final sample of 831 children. The final sample was nearly evenly split by gender (girls = 437, boys = 394). These children had normal nonverbal intelligence (M = 96.94, SD = 15.47, on the Kaufman Brief Intelligence Test-Second Edition [KBIT]; Kaufman & Kaufman, 2004).

Assessment measures

Language

We measured children's language skills using three subtests of the Test of Language Development-Primary: 4th edition (TOLD-P:4; Hammill & Newcomer, 2008a) and the Test of Language Development-Intermediate: 4th edition (TOLD-I:4; Hammill & Newcomer, 2008b). The TOLD-P:4 was administered to participants 7 years and younger, and the TOLD-I:4 was administered to children 8 years of age and older. Accordingly, participants in first and second grades were administered the Picture Vocabulary, Syntactic Understanding, and Morphological Completion subtests of the TOLD-P:4, and participants in third, fourth, and fifth grades were administered Picture Vocabulary, Sentence Combining, and Morphological Comprehension. Children 8 years old and older who were unable to achieve basal on the particular subtests of the TOLD-I:4 were administered the corresponding subtests of the TOLD-P:4 (e.g., Morphological Completion was administered in place of Morphological Comprehension). These subtests assess children's receptive vocabulary, syntax, and morphological knowledge. Although the selected subtests of the two versions of the TOLD measure similar constructs, the scoring is based on different scales.

Unfortunately, the two versions of the TOLD are not vertically scaled – a score on the TOLD-P:4 cannot be compared in a meaningful mathematical way to a score on the TOLD-I:4, except via norm-referenced standard scores (called *scaled scores* in the manual, with a mean of 10 and standard deviation of 3). To overcome this lack of an appropriate developmental scale in our longitudinal sample, we fit a single-factor model of language to the second-grade students in the study. Second-grade students are at the recommended age boundary between the versions of the test (8 years old), and depending on their performance they were administered the TOLD-P:4 or TOLD-I:4.

Our resulting sample of second-grade students included 205 who took three TOLD-P:4 subtests, 110 students who took three TOLD-I:4 subtests, and 16 students who took a mixture of subtests of each version. Because the intention of the TOLD is to measure general language ability, we fit a confirmatory single-factor model to all six subtests for second grade that treated the test scores as missing at random and jointly scaled all tests to indicate latent language ability. This model fit excellently – $\chi^2 = 3.78$, $df = 6$, comparative fit index (CFI) = 1.00, Tucker-Lewis index (TLI) = 1.02, root mean square error of approximation (RMSEA) < 0.01 – with good standardized loadings for the six subtests (median loading = 0.73). We then applied the parameters (loadings and intercepts) of this second-grade model to the full sample of students across all grades for the versions of the tests they took. This was a model of strong invariance (Meredith, 1993; Vandenberg & Lance, 2000) that allowed latent variances and means to be estimated across grades. The resulting factor scores indicated a longitudinally consistent z score of latent language ability, using whatever subtests or versions participants took (estimated via full information maximum likelihood). This developmental z score was the language score used in the current longitudinal study, with the mean and variance centered on second-grade performance.

Reading

Five subtests of the Woodcock-Johnson III Tests of Achievement (Mather, 2001) were used to assess children's ability to process and manipulate phonological information. Reading Vocabulary, Word Attack, Reading Fluency, Passage Comprehension, and Letter-Word Identification measure literacy and language-related skills that support reading.

Reliability

We established reliability by double-entering and scoring approximately 20% of the data obtained for all assessment instruments. Establishing entry reliability as well as scoring reliability was designed to ensure the quality and accuracy of data input. We calculated scores electronically using scoring tables that were created based on raw scores from the published scoring criteria. Agreement for entry reliability was 96%, and scoring reliability was 100% for the sample.

Administration and scoring procedures

All data were collected by trained master's- and doctoral-level students in communication disorders and related fields (e.g., education, developmental psychology, counseling psychology) under the direction of the project coordinators and principal investigators. Data collectors were from various racial/ethnic backgrounds and were speakers of American English. Data were collected in each child's school in quiet spaces identified for use by school personnel. Examiners received training on each instrument as presented in the examiner's manuals prior to collecting data in schools. Each instrument was scored by a second set of trained graduate students who were responsible for data reduction and who were supervised by project methodologists.

Research design

The larger project obtained 5-year longitudinal data from first-through fifth-grade African American students. An accelerated cohort design was used to test each participant across 2 years of the project. Specifically, in the first year of the project, we tested one cohort of participants, including 137 first graders, 134 second graders, 133 third graders, and 126 fourth graders; in the second year, we retested about 63% of these children, who were now second graders, third graders, fourth graders, and fifth graders. Meanwhile, in the second year, we also tested a new cohort of participants, including 127 first graders, 77 second graders, 90 third graders, 54 fourth graders, and 12 fifth graders; in the third year, we retested 41% of these children. Accordingly, 54% of the sample had two data points included in the data set. Children tested for the first time in fifth grade had only one data point. Table 2.1 shows the demographic characteristics of each cohort at each test occasion after we removed the 55 children involved in special education services and four children with missing gender information.

Table 2.1 Demographic characteristics by cohort (Wave 1).

Study year	Grade	Male (%)	Age		Intelligence	
			M	SD	M	SD
2013–2014	1	50	6.83	0.41	92.94	17.65
	2	40	7.88	0.49	96.51	15.17
	3	52	8.86	0.47	96.40	15.23
	4	48	9.96	0.57	95.32	13.58
2014–2015	1	45	6.86	0.48	97.56	14.70
	2	45	7.88	0.49	98.36	16.76
	3	47	8.77	0.46	102.82	14.82
	4	54	9.90	0.47	98.49	14.95
	5	58	11.33	0.60	97.75	9.26

Note: Intelligence is the standard score from the Kaufman Brief Intelligence Test. The table is given to describe the cohorts of the two-wave design, and intelligence and gender will be modeled longitudinally in subsequent results.

Data analysis

Although we were concerned with the academic performance of African American boys, the girls in the sample provided a natural comparison group, as they shared the same instruction and neighborhoods. Because this was a longitudinal sample, we used change score models to evaluate growth over time in Grades 1 to 5.

Change score models for growth

We used individual change score models to describe individual variability in intercept, proportional change, and constant change (the linear rate of change) in the form of dual change score models (McArdle, 2001; McArdle & Hamagami, 2001). We have used these models successfully to characterize the relationship between and growth in dialect variation and reading (Washington, Branum-Martin, Sun, & Lee-James, 2018). The general form of a dual change score model for a single outcome Y_{gi} for student i at grade g is as follows:

For $g = 1$,

$$Y_{1i} = Intercept_i + e_{1i} \tag{1}$$

For $g = 2$ to 5,

$$Y_{gi} = Y_{(g-1)i} + \Delta Y_{gi} + e_{gi} \tag{2}$$

$$\Delta Y_{gi} = \beta Y_{(g-1)i} + Slope_i \tag{3}$$

where *Intercept* is the student's individual starting point (i.e., the predicted initial score at Grade 1) and e_{1i} is random error (Eq. 1). Equation 2 shows how a student's score at any given time is a function of three things: the prior year's score ($Y_{(g-1)i}$), the amount of change (ΔY_{gi}), and random error (e_{gi}). Finally, Equation 3 describes the latent change score between the score at grade g (*Ygi*) and the score at grade (g-1) for each individual, which concludes the individual linear rate of change (*Slopes$_i$*, i.e., some students may grow faster than others) and the individual proportional change ($\beta Y_{(g-1)i}$), in which β is the proportional change parameter that describes the curvature of the growth trajectories. In addition, individual intercepts may covary with individual slopes.

The model is called *dual change* because of the linear growth combined with the proportional growth portion (Eq. 3). It can describe nonlinear trajectories with a proportional change parameter (fixed across individuals) that predicts status at any given time point as a function of the previous time point. Such a proportional change can be positive (accelerating growth, as in compound interest) or negative (decelerating growth, as in slowing to an asymptote). If the proportional change parameter happens to be zero, the change score model reduces to a model of individual linear growth.

The crucial test for the current study is that these growth models may differ between genders for all of the above parameters. Girls may start higher, grow faster, and have a different rate of proportional change – acceleration or deceleration may differ across genders. In addition, their variability may also differ: Girls may be more heterogeneous or homogeneous in intercepts and slopes than boys. Fortunately, these change score models can be readily tested across groups in a multiple-group structural equation modeling framework (Joreskog, 1970; Vandenberg & Lance, 2000; Little, 2013).

For each outcome, we present three models. First, we present an unrestricted (free) model for each of the two groups (i.e., a multiple-group structural equation modeling for growth). Second, because girls and boys might reasonably be expected to start schooling similarly, we present a model of equal initial status. Third, we present an omnibus model of no gender difference. We use this three-step process in order to isolate the nature of gender-based differences over time. If the third model of full equivalence fits, then there are no statistically dependable differences between boys and girls in their growth characteristics in this sample. If the third model fails but the second one fits, then girls and boys start equivalently but develop differently over time. Finally, if neither of these two restrictions fits, then girls and boys may differ in complex ways and should be evaluated separately, as if they each had their own growth model in Step 1.

Results

Table 2.2 presents descriptive statistics for boys and girls for each of the seven outcomes. Sample size, mean, standard deviation, skewness, and kurtosis are presented for each group. In addition, the two columns of difference present statistical tests of mean difference, with a t test and Cohen's d statistic for effect size. Most of the skewness and kurtosis values suggest that the performance did not deviate strongly from a normal shape. The rightmost two columns present the mean standard scores for each outcome for boys and girls. Five of the seven outcomes showed statistically significant ($p < .05$) mean differences favoring girls over boys. Regardless of statistical significance, the gender difference effect sizes for the reading outcomes ranged from 0.20 to 0.71 in Grades 4 to 5.

Table 2.2 Descriptive statistics.

Grade	Boys					Girls					Difference		Standard score	
	N	M	SD	Skewness	Kurtosis	N	M	SD	Skewness	Kurtosis	t	d	Boys	Girls
Kaufman Brief Intelligence Test, total score														
1	112	19.28	4.69	1.03	0.97	123	19.62	5.14	0.69	0.09	-0.53	.07	93.53	96.94
2	148	22.33	5.26	0.19	-0.85	184	22.65	5.56	0.20	-0.64	-0.53	.06	98.12	99.30
3	163	25.46	5.75	-0.20	-0.66	172	25.85	4.99	-0.15	-0.26	-0.67	.07	99.34	102.24
4	153	26.99	4.99	-0.29	-0.25	145	26.71	4.91	-0.44	-0.13	0.48	-.06	96.78	96.88
5	58	27.67	5.04	-0.02	-0.53	46	29.50	5.18	-0.44	1.36	-1.81	.36	92.56	97.27
Test of Language Development, factor score														
1	121	-0.55	0.95	-0.25	-0.10	127	-0.57	0.88	-0.05	-0.04	0.18	-.02	9.08	9.15
2	148	0.15	0.91	-0.02	-0.45	182	-0.05	0.97	0.16	-0.56	1.88	-.21	9.26	8.99
3	162	0.52	1.05	0.28	-0.52	172	0.32	1.11	0.36	-0.54	1.69	-.19	7.97	7.97
4	153	0.89	0.91	0.42	-0.29	144	0.86	1.00	0.18	-0.14	0.31	-.03	6.96	7.65
5	58	1.30	0.96	-0.07	-0.02	47	1.37	1.13	0.22	0.51	-0.33	.07	7.33	7.87
WJ Letter–Word Identification, W score														
1	122	430.75	30.48	0.49	0.30	128	435.31	28.20	0.14	0.49	-1.23	0.16	106.71	111.62
2	151	462.55	31.91	-0.28	-0.01	186	464.19	24.12	-0.02	-0.61	-0.52	0.06	103.01	104.65
3	167	483.40	25.25	-0.67	1.66	175	482.95	23.14	-0.99	2.03	0.17	-0.02	99.79	101.44
4	154	491.03	24.60	-0.41	0.55	145	495.50	18.62	-0.07	0.61	-1.78	0.20	96.90	99.89
5	59	498.32	24.19	-0.47	0.21	47	508.53	19.30	-0.50	-0.21	-2.36*	0.47	96.28	101.85

(Continued)

Table 2.2 (Continued)

Grade	Boys					Girls					Difference		Standard score	
	N	M	SD	Skewness	Kurtosis	N	M	SD	Skewness	Kurtosis	t	d	Boys	Girls
WJ Word Attack, W score														
1	122	465.87	25.65	-0.41	0.49	127	468.45	19.30	-0.76	2.54	0.89	0.11	109.02	113.39
2	151	480.97	21.33	-0.21	1.09	186	481.35	17.17	0.20	0.31	0.18	0.02	102.96	103.96
3	167	492.11	18.03	-0.13	0.71	174	489.56	16.77	-0.31	-0.04	-1.35	-0.15	100.80	100.48
4	154	492.62	19.72	-0.22	0.31	145	498.04	16.02	0.08	-0.44	2.61*	0.30	97.49	100.97
5	59	497.24	21.68	0.17	-0.61	47	505.83	16.38	0.29	-0.12	2.25*	0.44	98.36	102.98
WJ Reading Vocabulary, W score														
1	120	457.08	15.07	0.53	-0.73	128	460.92	16.16	0.56	-0.48	1.93	0.25	97.63	100.82
2	149	476.06	17.97	-0.13	-0.47	184	476.99	15.19	-0.13	-0.34	0.51	0.06	99.41	100.27
3	164	487.04	16.01	-0.15	0.11	171	486.55	14.49	-0.44	0.79	-0.29	-0.03	98.47	99.93
4	153	490.37	15.11	-0.20	0.65	145	493.63	13.78	0.07	0.47	1.94	0.23	95.37	98.03
5	57	495.51	11.67	-0.34	1.78	47	503.57	13.05	0.68	0.56	3.32*	0.66	92.58	101.34
WJ Passage Comprehension, W score														
1	122	450.80	21.77	-0.41	-0.49	128	455.48	18.68	-0.11	-0.26	-1.82	0.23	99.14	104.10
2	151	472.41	16.82	-0.57	0.21	186	473.56	13.13	-0.23	0.00	-0.69	0.08	97.54	98.87
3	167	481.16	12.84	-2.03	13.57	175	480.37	11.88	-0.99	3.10	0.60	-0.06	93.44	94.27
4	154	483.62	11.83	-0.46	0.73	145	485.74	9.66	-0.17	0.18	-1.70	0.20	88.97	91.54
5	59	487.20	9.32	-0.37	-0.03	47	493.40	9.25	-0.17	-0.52	-3.41*	0.67	86.74	92.32
WJ Reading Fluency, W score														
1	86	446.41	18.86	0.00	0.09	93	449.62	17.55	0.81	3.95	1.18	0.18	106.53	109.55
2	139	462.87	19.70	-0.05	0.74	180	464.54	16.30	0.02	1.05	0.81	0.09	100.31	102.33
3	162	474.89	16.82	0.50	0.05	168	476.41	14.33	-0.08	2.52	0.88	0.10	96.26	98.90
4	152	483.72	19.32	0.69	1.10	145	489.83	21.12	0.70	0.62	2.60*	0.30	93.84	97.79
5	57	490.44	19.98	0.57	-0.14	47	508.11	30.33	1.62	3.72	3.43*	0.71	91.44	99.46

Note: The expected standard score is 10 for the Test of Language Development and 100 for the other six outcomes.
WJ = Woodcock-Johnson III Tests of Achievement.
*$p < .05$, differences are scaled in favor of girls.

Growth model tests

Because these were longitudinal data, and many students appeared in two grades, these grade-wise differences can be better evaluated for what they suggest about growth over time. Table 2.3 presents the results of the three growth models for each of the seven outcomes. Table 2.3 presents conventional fit statistics, including chi-square, longitudinal CFI (Little, 2013), TLI, and RMSEA. Most models fit reasonably well overall (Little, 2013; Marsh, Hau, & Grayson, 2005; Marsh, Hau, & Wen, 2004) and are discussed in detail. The constrained models for each outcome also had nested model comparisons, including a p value for the chi-square difference (p[LRT]), the change in CFI (Cheung & Rensvold, 2002; Little, 2013; Marsh et al., 2005; Marsh et al., 2004), and the final column of Table 2.3 noting whether the model suggested gender equality for the parameters being tested.

For the tests of model restriction, the p value for the likelihood ratio test (p[LRT]) notes whether the model with parameters constrained to be equal across genders fits just as well as the freely estimated two-group model (i.e., $p > .05$ would suggest equality across genders). However, the LRT is noted to be rather conservative, rejecting constrained models that might otherwise be reasonable (Cheung & Rensvold, 2002). Therefore, we also report the change in CFI, in which a decrease greater than .010 indicates substantial misfit for the constraints or that there is a gender difference in the constrained parameters.

The free model had reasonable fit for most outcomes (CFI, TLI > .90, RMSEA < .10), which indicates that a dual change score model fit jointly to both genders was a reasonable characterization of the growth trajectories. Although there are no objective criteria for evaluating the fit of these longitudinal models (Little, 2013; Marsh et al., 2005; Marsh et al., 2004), the free model for KBIT and passage comprehension showed some misfit on TLI (less than .90). In addition, the free model for passage comprehension and reading vocabulary also showed some misfit, with RMSEAs of .109 and .107, respectively.

The first model restriction (Step 2) was to test for equal starting points across genders in first grade. The intercepts-equal model fit in an absolute sense (p[LRT] < .05) for five of the seven outcomes. The more reasonable test of ΔCFI fit for all seven outcomes (ΔCFI < − .010), which suggests that in the context of a longitudinal model of all five grades on average boys and girls perform similarly in first grade. The second model restriction, the omnibus test of total equality across genders (Step 3), fit in an absolute sense (p[LRT] < .05) for four of the seven outcomes. The more reasonable test of ΔCFI suggests that growth trajectories are completely equal across genders for all outcomes except passage comprehension and reading fluency (ΔCFI < − .010).

Table 2.3 Change score model tests of equality across genders.

Outcome	Model	χ^2	df	CFI	TLI	RMSEA	p(LRT)	ΔCFI	Gender equality
Kaufman Brief Intelligence Test	Free[a]	62.24	18	.909	.878	.078			
	Intercept equal[a]	62.25	20	.913	.895	.072	.995	.004	Yes
	All equal[a]	63.18	22	.915	.907	.068	.629	.002	Yes
Test of Language Development	Free[a]	26.36	18	.988	.984	.034			
	Intercept equal[a]	27.69	20	.989	.987	.031	.512	.001	Yes
	All equal[a]	31.53	22	.986	.985	.033	.147	−.003	Yes
WJ Letter-Word Identification	Free	54.66	14	.972	.952	.084			
	Intercept equal	56.49	16	.972	.958	.078	.402	.000	Yes
	All equal	70.59	20	.965	.958	.078	.007	−.007	Yes
WJ Word Attack	Free	40.59	14	.967	.944	.068			
	Intercept equal	49.90	16	.958	.937	.072	.009	−.009	Yes
	All equal	57.88	20	.953	.944	.068	.092	−.005	Yes
WJ Reading Vocabulary	Free[a]	102.31	18	.927	.903	.107			
	Intercept equal[a]	103.20	20	.928	.914	.101	.642	.001	Yes
	All equal[a]	116.69	22	.918	.911	.103	.001	−.010	Yes
WJ Passage Comprehension	Free[a]	106.35	18	.920	.894	.109			
	Intercept equal[a]	114.29	20	.915	.898	.107	.019	−.005	Yes
	All equal[a]	128.58	22	.904	.895	.109	.001	−.011	Not equal
WJ Reading Fluency	Free	34.03	14	.977	.961	.061			
	Intercept equal	39.69	16	.973	.959	.062	.059	−.004	Yes
	All equal	62.84	20	.951	.941	.075	.000	−.022	Not equal

Note: See the text for a discussion of model fit. CFI = comparative fit index. TLI = Tucker-Lewis index; RMSEA = root mean square error of approximation; p(LRT) = p value from the likelihood ratio test as a difference in chi-square versus the free model; ΔCFI = change in CFI versus the free model; WJ = Woodcock-Johnson III Tests of Achievement.

a Slope variance fixed at zero to achieve convergence for both genders.

Model results

The resulting parameters of these dual change score models (Eqs. 1–3) are presented in Tables 2.4 and 2.5. Table 2.4 presents the parameter estimates for the five outcomes that resulted in equality across genders (residual variances

Table 2.4 Model estimates for outcomes with equal growth parameters across genders.

Outcome	Parameter	Estimate	SE
Kaufman Brief Intelligence Test	Intercept mean	19.95	0.30
	Slope mean	3.64	0.64
	Proportional change	−0.06	0.03
	Intercept variance	18.25	2.33
	Slope variance	–	–
	Covariance (intercept, slope)	–	–
	Residual	12.43/11.64	1.21/1.06
Test of Language Development	Intercept mean	−0.55	0.05
	Slope mean	0.47	0.02
	Proportional change	0.03	0.02
	Intercept variance	0.63	0.06
	Slope variance	–	–
	Covariance (intercept, slope)	–	–
	Residual	0.24/0.23	0.02/0.02
WJ Letter–Word Identification	Intercept mean	21.77	0.08
	Slope mean	8.86	0.51
	Proportional change	−0.34	0.02
	Intercept variance	2.27	0.19
	Slope variance	0.17	0.03
	Covariance (intercept, slope)	0.25	0.06
	Residual	0.12/0.10	0.02/0.02
WJ Word Attack	Intercept mean	23.41	0.06
	Slope mean	8.16	1.13
	Proportional change	−0.32	0.05
	Intercept variance	1.03	0.10
	Slope variance	0.10	0.03
	Covariance (intercept, slope)	0.12	0.05
	Residual	0.18/0.11	0.02/0.02
WJ Reading Vocabulary	Intercept mean	23.09	0.05
	Slope mean	3.60	0.39
	Proportional change	−0.13	0.02
	Intercept variance	0.72	0.06
	Slope variance	–	–
	Covariance between intercept and slope	–	–
	Residual	0.11/0.11	0.01/0.01

Note: Estimates before the slash are for boys, and those after the slash are for girls (residual variances and their standard errors). Dashes indicate a parameter constrained to zero. WJ = Woodcock-Johnson III Tests of Achievement.

were allowed to differ; Little, 2013), including the model-predicted mean for intercept (status at first grade), slope (linear change), and proportional change. The variances of the intercept, slope, and residuals are given, along with the covariance, if applicable.

The first outcome in Table 2.4 shows the model estimates for intelligence (KBIT), with a total score of 19.95 items and a mean linear rate of change of 3.64 items per year. The proportional change was −0.06, which indicates that growth decelerated by 6% per year. The intercept variance of 18.25 suggests that there was wide variability (SD = 4.3 items) in first grade. There was no estimable variance in slope, which suggests that students grew in parallel trajectories. The TOLD was estimated on a factor score (z scale) centered at second grade. The intercept mean of −0.55, combined with mean slope of 0.47, suggests that first graders started about 0.5 SD below second graders ($z \approx 0$) and grew an average of nearly 0.5 SD per year. Proportional change was fairly close to zero (3%), which suggests mostly linear change.

The three Woodcock-Johnson tests in Table 2.4 were on a W score, but in order to get model convergence, we rescaled them by dividing by 20 points (this linear transformation did not change statistical features of the model or substantive interpretation). Letter-word identification and word attack had similar intercept, slope, and proportional change estimates (−0.34 and −0.32, respectively, suggesting decelerating growth). Both had estimated slope variances, and the covariance indicated a positive relation between intercept and slope (r = .39 for letter-word identification and r = .37 for word attack), which suggests that students who started higher grew faster. Reading vocabulary in Table 2.4 had a mean intercept of 23.09 (SD = 0.84) with a mean slope of 3.6 units and a proportional change of −13%. There was no estimable variance in slopes.

Table 2.5 presents results for the dual change score models for the two outcomes that had gender differences: passage comprehension and reading fluency. The layout of the table is similar to that of Table 2.4 but with separate columns for each gender. For passage comprehension, the mean slope for boys was 6.88 units, whereas for girls it was 8.38. The proportional change parameters were also fairly different: −27% for boys and −34% for girls. The results for reading fluency in Table 2.5 suggest strong difference in growth. The mean slope was 3.89 units for boys and 0.66 for girls. The proportional change parameter was −.14 for boys and almost zero (.003) for girls.

Visualizing the model implications

Because these dual change score models are complex, they are best interpreted visually – especially for the models in which multiple parameters

Table 2.5 Model parameter estimates for outcomes with unequal growth parameters across genders.

Outcome	Parameter	Boys		Girls	
		Estimate	SE	Estimate	SE
WJ Passage Comprehension	Proportional change	−0.27	0.02	−0.34	0.02
	Intercept mean	22.80	0.05	22.80	0.05
	Slope mean	6.88	0.53	8.38	0.50
	Intercept variance	1.04	0.09	1.04	0.09
	Slope variance	–	–	–	–
	Covariance (intercept, slope)	–	–	–	–
	Residual	0.14	0.02	0.12	0.01
WJ Reading Fluency	Proportional change	−0.14	0.06	0.00	0.05
	Intercept mean	22.40	0.06	22.40	0.06
	Slope mean	3.89	1.32	0.66	1.25
	Intercept variance	0.72	0.10	0.72	0.10
	Slope variance	0.07	0.03	0.17	0.03
	Covariance (intercept, slope)	0.00	0.07	−0.25	0.06
	Residual	0.19	0.03	0.19	0.03

Note: Dashes indicate a parameter constrained to zero. WJ= Woodcock-Johnson III Tests of Achievement.

differ across groups. Figures 2.1–2.3 show growth plots for each of the five outcomes that did not show gender differences. Figure 2.1 shows KBIT (top) and language (TOLD; at bottom), each with a gray line for each student in the two-wave accelerated cohort design. Each plot also has a dark line for the predicted average from the dual change score model. These graphs are helpful in that the simultaneous effects of the linear and proportional change parameters are shown. Figure 2.1 shows that average growth in both intelligence and language appears essentially linear in Grades 1 to 5.

Figure 2.2 presents individual student results (gray) and model-based predictions for letter-word identification (top) and word attack (bottom). Both panels present a slight deceleration over time. Figure 2.3 presents student data and model predictions for reading vocabulary, also showing slight deceleration but no difference across genders. Figure 2.4 presents the growth plots for the two outcomes that showed gender differences. Passage comprehension at the top of Figure 2.4 shows girls growing slightly faster than boys, with both having a deceleration. Reading fluency at the bottom of Figure 2.4 shows a high degree of similarity in the early grades, but while the girls grow essentially linearly, boys have substantial deceleration, evident by fifth grade.

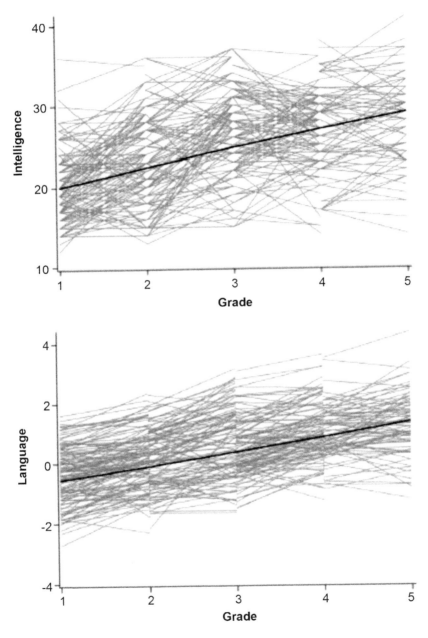

Figure 2.1 Individual growth plot with model-predicted change line for intelligence (top) and language (bottom).

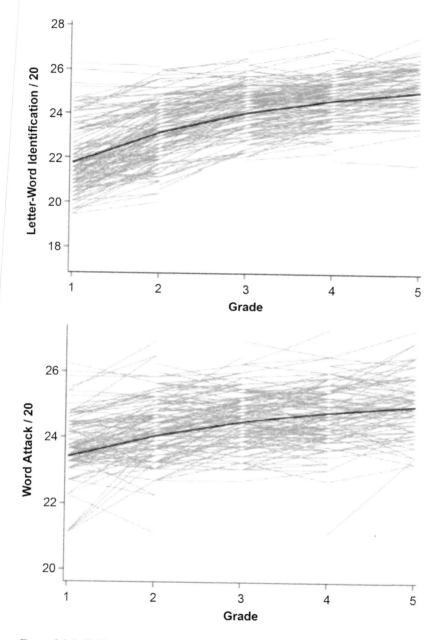

Figure 2.2 Individual growth plot with model-predicted change line for WJ Letter-Word Identification (top) and WJ Word Attack (bottom). WJ = Woodcock-Johnson III Tests of Achievement.

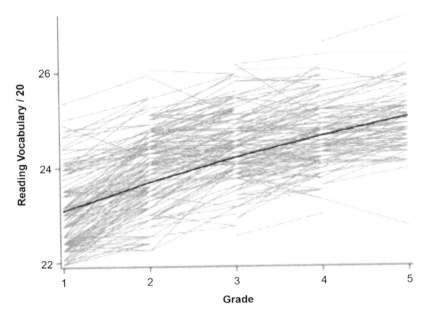

Figure 2.3 Individual growth plot with model-predicted change line for Woodcock-Johnson III Tests of Achievement Reading Vocabulary.

Discussion

Using a longitudinal, accelerated cohort design, we examined the performance of African American children on language and reading measures across first through fifth grades. Overall, the outcomes demonstrated that there was no evidence of gender differences in language or cognition in first through fifth grades. For reading comprehension and fluency, boys and girls performed equally in the early grades (i.e., first through third grades), but differences by gender emerged in fourth and/or fifth grade. Findings for language suggested that boys and girls performed equally. There were no statistically significant performance differences by gender. Furthermore, growth models indicated that African American boys and girls evidenced similar growth trajectories for language in first through fifth grades as well. These findings support the results of an early meta-analysis by Hyde and Linn (1988) that demonstrated that even when gender differences were apparent in language skills, the magnitude of the difference was so small as to be considered insignificant or nonexistent.

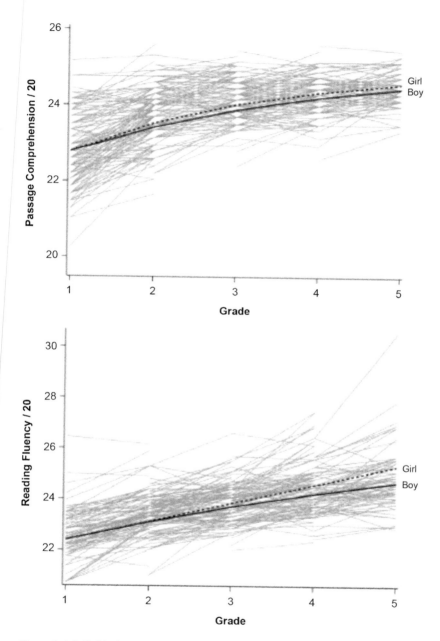

Figure 2.4 Individual growth plot with model-predicted change line for WJ Passage
Comprehension (top) and WJ Reading Fluency (bottom). WJ = Woodcock-
Johnson III Tests of Achievement.

The results of the current investigation support the statement that these differences simply do not exist. Maccoby and Jacklin (1974), in contrast, performed a meta-analysis of 85 articles focused on gender and language and reported a pattern such that girls and boys were similar or equal early on language skills, but in preadolescence (~10 years of age) and beyond these skills diverged, with significant deceleration evident for boys. That pattern was not identified in the current sample of African American boys and girls for language, but it was apparent for reading. Instead, our outcome for language supports the 70% of studies reviewed by Maccoby and Jacklin (1974) that showed no differences in linguistic development for boys and girls.

It is important to note that the children in the current investigation were older than those included in many studies focused on gender differences in language. Studies with younger participants report that gender differences are apparent in infancy, toddlerhood, and preschool but disappear by kindergarten (Aratani et al., 2011; Bauer et al., 2002; Eriksson et al., 2012; Iruka et al., 2014; Maccoby & D'Andrade, 1966). Perhaps that was true for the participants in this investigation who showed no evidence of gender differences in language performance or growth by first grade.

Our findings contrast with the small number of studies focused specifically on gender differences in the language skills of African American children (Mainess et al., 2012; Roberts et al., 1999). These investigations, which were focused on preschoolers (Roberts et al., 1999) and preadolescents (Mainess et al., 2012), suggest that the language of African American girls is more varied and complex than that of African American boys and that these differences persist (Aratani et al., 2011). All of these investigations were focused on the performance of boys (and girls) from low-income homes. The current sample included largely low-income participants as well.

The Mainess et al. (2012) and Roberts et al. (1999) investigations both had small sample sizes; thus, it is possible that the variability in the language performance of their participants led to findings that would not be replicated with a larger sample with more power to detect both similarities and differences in performance. Perhaps important as well, though the current investigation and these earlier ones all examined gender differences in language, the language skills targeted were different. It is possible that with language, as is true with reading, gender differences can exist in the development of specific language skills or domains but not others (Tomblin et al., 1997). Aratani et al. (2011), though focused on African American boys, studied the race gap in achievement, which has a strong evidence base that suggests that these differences persist in all domains when African American boys are compared to their White and Asian peers.

Reading skill performance and growth in selected reading skills differed by gender in that reading trajectories diverged over time. No gender differences were apparent for any of the five reading skills measured in Grades 1–3. Gender differences in the descriptive statistics were not always consistent across these skills in Grades 4 and 5. Specifically, statistically significant differences in favor of girls were apparent in Grades 4 and 5 for reading fluency and word attack and in Grade 5 only for letter-word identification, passage comprehension, and reading vocabulary. Several other investigations have reported that the reading gap between boys and girls becomes apparent with advancing grade. Several have identified secondary school as the time at which this gap becomes apparent (Caro et al., 2009; Kingdon et al., 2017; Logan & Johnston, 2010; Voyer & Voyer, 2014). The growth models used suggest that not all of these observed differences are dependable, as girls differed from boys only on reading comprehension and reading fluency. Further longitudinal research could help to clarify which of these observed differences persist, grow, or disappear.

The current investigation documented gender differences in reading abilities that emerged earlier than secondary school; the boys' reading performance began to diverge as early as fourth grade. It is important to note that several of the skills on which African American boys showed decline in both fourth and fifth grades were skills that have been identified as early literacy skills that are foundational to becoming a good reader in later grades (Scarborough, 2001). Specifically, word attack and letter-word identification are critical for reading at the word level. As a result, they are both often the intense focus of early literacy programs. Perhaps most important, these skills support the development of more advanced reading skills, such as comprehension and fluency (Archer, Gleason, & Vachon, 2003; Cutting & Scarborough, 2006; Scarborough, 2001). Accordingly, weaknesses in these key early literacy skills would likely not provide a strong enough reading foundation to support the more complex reading required in fourth and fifth grades, in which content vocabulary is greater and the reading material becomes more syntactically complex and abstract. Thus, though boys performed only slightly below the mean on the TOLD and there were no gender differences, their early literacy skills appear not to be sufficiently strong to support the development of later reading abilities such as comprehension and fluency that rely on these early language skills.

Individual growth modeling also showed that the African American boys in this investigation experienced consistent growth in reading skills in the early grades, with divergence from girls occurring in the upper grades. Growth trajectories were essentially equal across genders for all outcomes except passage comprehension and reading fluency. Specifically, on the passage comprehension task, girls grew slightly faster than boys, but both boys and girls showed evidence of deceleration. With respect to reading fluency, girls were observed to grow linearly, whereas boys had substantial deceleration in fifth grade. This pattern has been described in the literature, whereby the reading trajectory for girls progresses more quickly and the trajectory for boys slows rapidly with age. Research suggests that this is the beginning of a gap in performance by gender (and SES) that will continue to widen with increasing age and grade (Kingdon et al., 2017; Logan & Johnston, 2010).

There are perhaps other variables that influence these outcomes for African American boys that were not considered in this investigation. Several, including motivation, the development of learning-related skills (e.g., executive function and social skills), differential interest in reading, gender-relevant curriculum content, and externalizing behaviors, among others, have been implicated (Bristol, 2015; Davis, 2003; Husband, 2012b; Matthews et al., 2010; McClelland et al., 2006). A likely explanation based on the trends identified in this study is that these boys simply have developed weak overall reading skills that catch up with them in later grades; reading comprehension and fluency become casualties of these weaknesses. In order to become skilled readers students must be able to connect their early literacy skills to later reading ability (Scarborough, 2001).

Scarborough (2001) divided reading skills into strands that early readers must master. According to Scarborough, most children who struggle with reading exhibit difficulty with mastery of the word recognition strand, which includes skills like phonemic and phonological awareness and letter-word identification. This pattern of reading difficulty characterizes the performance of the African American boys in the current investigation. Scarborough further suggested that later reading difficulty is often related to weaknesses in preschool language skills, even when these skills appear to resolve in later grades. This is particularly true for children for whom there is a family history of reading difficulty. In the current investigation, boys and girls performed and grew equally on measures of syntax, semantics, and morphology, which suggests that language differences did not differentiate the children in this sample, though this may have been true at younger ages. Furthermore, growth in language and reading related to the use of African American English dialect was examined using this same sample of 831 children (Washington et al, 2018). Though dialect use impacted reading, no gender differences were observed.

Why are these differences apparent for African American boys but not girls? This is the question that we all seek to answer. School-related variables are often used to explain these differences. In particular, quality of the school environment and teacher quality are often implicated in the poor performance of boys. However, the boys and girls in this investigation were recruited from the same schools, neighborhoods, and classrooms and were exposed to similar teaching and classroom environments. The SES backgrounds of the students were also similar. Perhaps it is some of the social variables discussed by others at the child level related to issues such as motivation and interest in reading, curriculum content, or contextual variables related to disciplinary practices and expectations that could differ across genders.

These variables may be explanatory to some extent, but they were not examined in the current investigation and thus are beyond our current scope. What is clear is that the pattern of gender differences and growth for African American boys is very similar to that reported in the larger literature for non-African American students whose reading achievement is driven by mastery of word-level abilities. Furthermore, the pattern of reading skill weaknesses identified for African American boys mirrors those identified for most children who struggle with reading, as indicated by Scarborough (2001). These outcomes suggest that a reading instructional strategy that focuses specifically on these foundational literacy skills may be needed to improve the outlook for this population of students.

Conclusions and limitations

The purpose of this investigation was to characterize growth in and the development of reading and language skills among African American boys and to identify any existing gender differences in their performance compared to girls. Boys and girls performed similarly on language and intelligence tasks, but there were clear differences in reading-related measures always favoring girls. Growth trajectories for reading also differentiated boys and girls in fifth grade. An important overall finding is that the patterns of language and reading growth observed for African American boys were similar to the patterns reported for the general population of students who struggle with reading, which suggests that improving access to current interventions utilized with these students should be beneficial for African American boys as well. Research suggests that the deceleration of reading skills identified among African American boys at fourth and fifth grades will continue. Future research should focus on reading and language growth beyond elementary school. Though there may be underlying social and motivational concerns contributing to these outcomes, as has been suggested in the extant literature, future research focused on the development of strong reading pedagogy and interventions would benefit these boys.

A limitation of the current study is that the primary aims were to characterize reading, so only one measure of cognition and one measure of language were used. Although reading was well covered by multiple measures, future research may help substantiate the current findings by using more varied measures of cognition and language. Multivariate models relating change across outcomes and their mutual, longitudinal influence may also be informative. Another limitation of the current investigation is that performance by classroom was not considered. Although six of the seven schools in the current sample were highly similar to one another in terms of racial makeup (>90% of students were African American) and low-income status (>90% of students qualified for free or reduced-price lunch), differences across classrooms may explain some of the variability. However, because students change classrooms yearly (are cross-classified), it is unclear how such variability would contribute to the shape of dual change score models (and most software cannot handle such cross-classified nesting in a multivariate 5-year model).

Although the accelerated cohort design yields 5 years of longitudinal data, no child was measured on more than two occasions. The overall shape of the trajectories may be adequately captured, but variability and individual differences in shape are poorly estimated. Future research with longer term designs and more measurement points may better explain individual variation in trajectories and provide stronger across-group comparisons (see Caro et al., 2009, for a cogent discussion of this point). Finally, the current sample ended at Grade 5. Further research would be helpful to determine whether the current trends stabilize, diverge, or disappear in later grades.

References

Anastasi, A. (1958). Heredity, environment, and the question how? *Psychological Review, 65*(4), 197.

Aratani, Y., Wight, V. R., & Cooper, J. L. (2011). Racial Gaps in Early Childhood: Socio-emotional Health, Developmental, and Educational Outcomes Among African-American Boys. Retrieved from Malman School of Public Health:

Archer, A. L., Gleason, M. M., & Vachon, V. L. (2003). Decoding and fluency: Foundation skills for struggling older readers. *Learning Disability Quarterly, 26*(2), 89–101.

Bauer, D. J., Goldfield, B. A., & Reznick, J. S. (2002). Alternative approaches to analyzing individual differences in the rate of early vocabulary development. *Applied Psycholinguistics, 23*, 313–335.

Bohrnstedt, G., Kitmitto, S., Ogut, B., Sherman, D., & Chan, D. (2015). School Composition and the Black-White Achievement Gap. Retrieved from Washington, DC: http://nces.ed.gov/pubsearch

Bristol, T. J. (2015). Teaching boys: Towards a theory of gender-relevant pedagogy. *Gender and Education, 27*(1), 53–68.

Caro, D. H., McDonald, J. T., & Willms, J. D. (2009). Socioeconomic status and academic achievement trajectories from childhood to adolescence. *Canadian Journal of Education, 32*(3), 558–590.

Chatterji, M. (2006). Reading Achievement Gaps, Correlates, and Moderators of Early Reading Achievement: Evidence From the Early Childhood Longitudinal

Study (ECLS) Kindergarten to First Grade Sample. *Journal of Educational Psychology*, *98*(3), 489–507.

Cheung, G. W., & Rensvold, R. B. (2002). Evaluating goodness-of-fit indexes for testing measurement invariance. *Structural Equation Modeling: A Multidisciplinary Journal*, *9*(2), 233–255.

Connell, J. P., Spencer, M. B., & Aber, J. L. (1994). Educational risk and resilience in African-American youth: Context, self, action, and outcomes in school. *Child development*, *65*(2), 493–506.

Curby, T. W., Rimm-Kaufman, S. E., & Ponitz, C. C. (2009). Teacher-child interactions and children's achievement trajectories across kindergarten and first grade. *Journal of Educational Psychology*, *101*(4), 912.

Cutting, L. E., & Scarborough, H. S. (2006). Prediction of reading comprehension: Relative contributions of word recognition, language proficiency, and other cognitive skills can depend on how comprehension is measured. *Scientific Studies of Reading*, *10*(3), 277–299.

Davis, J. E. (2003). Early schooling and academic achievement of African American males. *Urban Education*, *38*(5), 515–537.

Eriksson, M., Marschik, P. B., Tulviste, T., Almgren, M., Pérez Pereira, M., Wehberg, S.,... Gallego, C. (2012). Differences between girls and boys in emerging language skills: evidence from 10 language communities. *British Journal of Developmental Psychology*, *30*(2), 326–343. doi:10.1111/j.2044-835X.2011.02042.x

Fantuzzo, J., LeBoeuf, W., Rouse, H., & Chen, C.-C. (2012). Academic achievement of African American boys: A city-wide, community-based investigation of risk and resilience. *Journal of School Psychology*, *50*(5), 559–579. doi:10.1016/j.jsp.2012.04.004

Flannery, K. A., Liederman, J., Daly, L., & Schultz, J. (2000). Male prevalence for reading disability is found in a large sample of black and white children free from ascertainment bias. *Journal of the International Neuropsychological Society*, *6*(4), 433–442.

Hammill, D. D., & Newcomer, P. L. (2008a). *Test of language development-primary*, 4th Edition. Austin, TX: Pro-Ed.

Hammill, D. D., & Newcomer, P. L. (2008b). *Test of language development-intermediate*, 4th Edition. Austin, TX: Pro-Ed.

Harris, T. S., & Graves, S. L. Jr, (2010). The influence of cultural capital transmission on reading achievement in African American fifth grade boys. *Journal of Negro Education*, *79* (4), 447–457.

Husband, T. (2012a). Addressing reading underachievement in African American boys through a Multi-Contextual approach. *Reading Horizons*, *52*(1), 1–25.

Husband, T. (2012b). Why can't Jamal read? *Phi Delta Kappan*, *93*(5), 23–27.

Huttenlocher, J., Haight, W., Bryk, A., Seltzer, M., & Lyons, T. (1991). Early vocabulary growth: Relation to language input and gender. *Developmental Psychology*, *27*(2), 236–248.

Hyde, J. S., & Linn, M. C. (1988). Gender differences in verbal ability: A meta-analysis. *Psychological Bulletin*, *104* (1), 53–69. doi:10.1037/0033-2909.104.1.53

Iruka, I. U. (2017). Perception is not always reality. *Exchange (19460406)*, *39*(234), 46–47.

Iruka, I. U., Gardner-Neblett, N., Matthews, J. S., & Winn, D.-M. C. (2014). Preschool to kindergarten transition patterns for African American boys. *Early Childhood Research Quarterly*, *29*(2), 106–117. doi:10.1016/ j.ecresq.2013.11.004

Jencks, C., & Phillips, M. (2011). *The Black-White test score gap.* Washington, DC: Brookings Institution Press.

Jöreskog, K. G. (1970). A general method for estimating a linear structural equation system. *ETS Research Bulletin Series, 1970*(2), i–41.

Justice, L. M., Invernizzi, M., Geller, K., Sullivan, A. K., & Welsch, J. (2005). Descriptive-developmental performance of at-risk preschoolers on early literacy tasks. *Reading Psychology, 26*(1), 1–25.

Kaufman, A. S., & Kaufman, N. L. (2004). *Kaufman Brief Intelligence Test* 2nd Edition. Bloomington, MN: Pearson.

Kidd, E., & Lum, J. A. G. (2008). Sex differences in past tense overregularization. *Developmental Science, 11*(6), 882–889. doi:10.1111/j.1467-7687.2008.00744.x

Kingdon, D., Serbin, L. A., & Stack, D. M. (2017). Understanding the gender gap in school performance among low-income children: A developmental trajectory analysis. *International Journal of Behavioral Development, 41*(2), 265–274.

Liederman, J., Kantrowitz, L., & Flannery, K. (2005). Male vulnerability to reading disability is not likely to be a myth: a call for new data. *Journal of Learning Disabilities, 38*(2), 109–129.

Little, T. D. (2013). *Longitudinal structural equation modeling.* New York, NY: Guilford Press.

Logan, S., & Johnston, R. (2010). Investigating gender differences in reading. *Educational Review, 62* (2), 175–187.

Maccoby, E. E., & D'Andrade, R. G. (1966). *The development of sex differences (Vol.5).* Redwood City, CA: Stanford University Press.

Maccoby, E. E., & Jacklin, C. N. (1974). Myth, reality and shades of gray: What we know and don't know about sex differences. *Psychology Today, 8*(7), 109–112.

Mainess, K. J., Champion, T. B., & McCabe, A. (2002). Narration by African American Preadolescents-Preliminary Examination of Gender and Socioeconomic Issues. *Linguistics and Education, 13*(2), 151–173.

Marsh, H. W., Hau, K.-T., & Grayson, D. (2005). Goodness of fit in structural equation models. In A. Maydeu-Olivares & J. J. McArdle (Eds.), *Contemporary psychometrics: A festschrift for Roderick P. McDonald* (pp. 275–340). Mahwah, NJ: Lawrence Erlbaum.

Marsh, H. W., Hau, K.-T., & Wen, Z. (2004). In search of golden rules: Comment on hypothesis-testing approaches to setting cutoff values for fit indexes and dangers in overgeneralizing Hu and Bentler's (1999) findings. *Structural Equation Modeling: A Multidisciplinary Journal, 11* (3), 320–341. doi:10.1207/s15328007sem1103_2

Mather, N. (2001). Woodcock-Johnson III tests of achievement: Examiner's manual: Riverside Pub.

Matthews, J. S., Kizzie, K. T., Rowley, S. J., & Cortina, K. (2010). African Americans and Boys: Understanding the Literacy Gap, Tracing Academic Trajectories and Evaluation the Role of Learning-Related Skills. *Journal of Educational Psychology, 102*(3), 757–771.

McArdle, J. J. (2001). A latent difference score approach to longitudinal dynamic structural analyses. In R. Cudeck, S. H. C. du Toit, & D. Sörbom (Eds.), *Structural equation modeling: Present and future* (pp. 342–380). Lincolnwood, IL: Scientific Software International

McArdle, J. J., & Hamagami, F. (2001). Latent difference score structural models for linear dynamic analyses with incomplete longitudinal data. In L. M. Collins & A. G. Sayer (Eds.), *New methods for the analysis of change* (pp. 139–175). Washington, DC: American Psychological Association.

McClelland, M. M., Acock, A. C., & Morrison, F. J. (2006). The impact of kindergarten learning-related skills on academic trajectories at the end of elementary school. *Early Childhood Research Quarterly, 21*(4), 471–490.

McGeown, S., Goodwin, H., Henderson, N., & Wright, P. (2012). Gender differences in reading motivation: does sex or gender identity provide a better account? *Journal of Research in Reading, 35*(3), 328–336.

McMillian, M. M., Frierson, H. T., & Campbell, F. A. (2011). Do gender differences exist in the academic identification of African American elementary school-aged children? *Journal of Black Psychology, 37*(1), 78–98.

Meredith, W. (1993). Measurement invariance, factor analysis, and factorial invariance. *Psychometrika, 58*(4), 525–543.

Raag, T., Kusiak, K., Tumilty, M., Kelemen, A., Bernheimer, H., & Bond, J. (2011). Reconsidering SES and gender divides in literacy achievement: are the gaps across social class and gender necessary? *Educational Psychology, 31*(6), 691–705.

Roberts, J. E., Burchinal, M., & Durham, M. (1999). Parents' report of vocabulary and grammatical development of African American preschoolers: child and environmental associations. *Child Development, 70*(1), 92–106.

Scarborough, H. S. (2001). Connecting early language and literacy to later reading (Dis) abilities: Evidence, theory and practice. In S. B. Neurman & D. K. Dickinson (Eds.), *Handbook of Early Literacy* (pp. 97–110). New York: Guilford Press.

Shaywitz, S. E., Shaywitz, B. A., Fletcher, J. M., & Escobar, M. D. (1990). Prevalence of reading disability in boys and girls: Results of the Connecticut Longitudinal Study. *JAMA, 264*(8), 998–1002.

Tamis-LeMonda, C. S., Song, L., Leavell, A. S., Kahana-Kalman, R., & Yoshikawa, H. (2012). Ethnic differences in mother-infant language and gestural communications are associated with specific skills in infants. *Developmental Science, 15*(3), 384–397. doi:10.1111/j.1467-7687.2012.01136.x

Tomblin, J. B., Records, N. L., Buckwalter, P., Zhang, X., Smith, E., & O'Brien, M. (1997). Prevalence of specific language impairment in kindergarten children. *Journal of Speech Language and Hearing Research, 40*(6), 1245–1260.

Vandenberg, R. J., & Lance, C. E. (2000). A review and synthesis of the measurement invariance literature: Suggestions, practices, and recommendations for organizational research. *Organizational Research Methods, 3*(1), 4–69.

Voyer, D., & Voyer, S. D. (2014). Gender differences in scholastic achievement: A meta-analysis. *Psychological Bulletin, 140*(4), 1174.

Washington, J. A., Branum-Martin, L., Sun, C., & Lee-James, R. (2018). The impact of dialect density on the growth of language and reading in African American children. *Language Speech and Hearing Services in Schools, 49*(2), 232–247. doi:10.1044/2018_LSHSS-17-0063

3 Exploring the master narrative

Racial knowledge and understanding of language and literacy pedagogy for special education teacher candidates

Joy Banks and Simone Gibson

As teacher educators, we seek to empower our preservice teachers with varying forms of cultural capital to help ensure their academic and career-based success (Lareau, 1987). Our preservice teachers seem to recognize lessons around social capital, often only after being provided with foundational knowledge regarding the genesis of the social systems that influence inequitable out-comes for marginalized people. Thus, it is important to understand dominant forms of cultural capital. As a means of providing foundational knowledge regarding multi-dialecticism, or forms of cultural capital related to speech, we engaged preservice teachers around Geneva Smitherman's (1977) and Lisa Delpit and Dowdy's (2006) work, which explores connections between language and power dynamics that influence inequitable academic and social outcomes for many African American learners. In response, one teacher candidate wrote,

> On a personal note, I had no idea about the history of black dialect. In the past, my impression was that in order for students to get ahead in the world they must speak the "Queen's English." I still think that is the case, but I now see that there are other ways for students to communicate effectively without losing their identity.

Too often teachers lack the preparation and exposures needed to address mindsets related to speech such as those reflected in the student quote above. Rather than simply focusing on conformity and denigrating the primary, yet nondominant, speaking cultures of marginalized populations of learners, teachers have the ability to disrupt negative, yet dominant, assumptions about intellect connected to the use of nonstandard English dialects, such as African American English (AAE).

The aforementioned teacher candidate quote served as motivation for the inception of this article, which advocates for educating preservice teachers to explore the master narrative, which useslanguage to denigrate the learning potential of marginalized of AA children, particularly AA boys. Without knowledge of the foundations and structures of language, the histories of diverse language differences, the myth of Standard English, or how language is difficult to disentangle from race, social class, and gender, among other social constructs, teachers may unknowingly embrace teaching pedagogies that favor speakers of American English (AE) at the expense of speakers of diverse forms of English, such as AAE. The lack of knowledge regarding language differences contributes to the cycles of underperformance for AA males. Teacher education programs have a responsibility to ensure that preservice teachers understand the ways in which power dynamics related to language intersect with race and class to marginalize students so that they in turn can learn to challenge this hegemonic language system and learn to empower students through critical teaching pedagogies.

Significance

Although some embrace the perspective that content knowledge is the only expertise needed to effectively engage in the teaching and learning processes, many educators and researchers alike understand the significance of developing teaching pedagogies (Bacon, Banks, Young, & Jackson, 2007; Shulman, 1986; Shulman & Shulman, 2004). Pedagogy involves the subconscious beliefs that influence a teacher's interactions with content, students, and the presentation of information (Freire, 1970; Giroux, 1997). Although it is time consuming and tedious, many teacher education programs attempt to address this task by helping teacher candidates to explore content (Koehler, Mishra, Kereluik, Shin, & Graham, 2013; Sanders-Smith & Gaumer, 2016; Wilkinson et al., 2017; Paige & Hardy, 2018) and a plethora of terms that fall under the diversity moniker (Adams & Bell, 2015; Ladson-Billings, 1999). Despite these efforts, engagement with preservice teachers around language diversity for AA learners is often missing from courses of study that are aligned with teacher certification. This is problematic because teachers' perceptions of language diversity play an indelible role in the ways in which speakers of nonstandard English are perceived, viewed, and treated by teachers, which in turn influence learning outcomes for AA students (Labov, 1969; Rickford, 1999; Dyson & Smitherman, 2009).

This article provides a conceptual overview regarding the need to prepare preservice teachers around the ways in which language is used to disempower AA males through the creation of a teaching framework. Our challenge is to cypher the varying bodies of research related to AAE from different research bases such as speech and language, multicultural education, urban education, history, and sociology. The goal of the framework is to ensure that preservice teachers are gaining access to exposures that might help them to understand and disrupt cycles of castigating AA males based on their speech. In so doing, this article connects the ways in which speech contributes to the matrices of social constructs (e.g., race, class, and gender) that are used to elevate some and disempower others. In addition, the significance of this article is in how it serves as a call to action for teacher education programs to prepare preservice teachers to understand the ways in which myths regarding SAE are used against marginalized learners in the same ways that race, class, and gender are used to diminish the potential of children. Although important, this topic is largely overlooked within the teacher education research literature.

In addition, this article seeks to bolster understandings regarding the ways in which language knowledge contributes to the matrices of social constructs that are used to elevate some and disempower others. We intentionally use the voices of special education teacher candidates to demonstrate the importance of the intersection between cultural and language knowledge for preservice teachers as an impetus for improving the reading performance of AA students and potentially reducing the overrepresentation of AA boys labeled as students with language and reading disabilities.

The need for the master narrative framework

Language is a seemingly innocuous element of learning that reflects the basic necessity of communication. This perspective is problematic. Language is a divisive tool that contributes to a belief system that marginalizes AA males. There is a misconception that language reflects intellect. Teachers too often perpetuate this misconception within schools as standards of SAE are reinforced at the expense of other dialects. Teacher education programs have a unique responsibility to help address the misconceptions that link dialect usage and intelligence. Ultimately, teachers' assumptions about students influence their interactions with students. If a teacher holds a negative perception of a child, his or her interactions with the child will reflect that negative perception. This in turn will contribute to that child forming negative perceptions of himself or herself, possessing lower aspirations compared to classmates, and underperforming academically. Although varying social constructs, such as race and social class, play a more apparent role in the ways in which teachers interact with students (Rist, 1970), language and dialect use also contribute to teachers' assumptions about children's intellectual abilities (Blanchett, Klingner, & Harry, 2003; Cross, DeVaney, & Jones, 2001; Fogel & Ehri, 2006; Godley, Reaser, & Moore, 2015).

Teacher education programs have a unique responsibility to expose pre-service teachers to the ways in which speech is used to uphold hegemonies that create inequalities for AA males. For starters, teacher candidates need greater training related to differences between multilingualism and multi-dialecticism. *Multilingual* typically refers to students who qualify as English language learners and speak multiple and different languages. *Multi-dialecticism* refers to variations of a single language. There are a multitude of variations of the English language. However, some dialects, such as SAE, are valued over nonstandard dialects, such as AAE. Beyond being exposed to these concepts associated with language, teachers need greater exposure to the myth that proper English exists (Alim, Rickford, & Ball, 2016; Charity-Hudley & Mallinson, 2010; Debose, 2007; Delpit & Dowdy, 2006; Fogel & Ehri, 2006; Hill, 2008). Although a plethora of research studies exist exploring the rules associated with varying dialects, including AAE, the myth of SAE superiority still persists (Wolfram, 2011; Dyson & Smitherman, 2009; Labov, 1972; Rickford, 1999).

As a consequence, teachers are in need of preparation, especially when interacting with AA males, to acknowledge how speech serves as one of the first devices used by teachers to denigrate the intelligence, cultures, and historical identities of marginalized children (Hilliard, 1983). When teacher candidates hear a nonstandard variation of English, they often "have been unprepared to understand the language phenomena which they observe" (p. 26) and rely on popularized yet unproven assumptions that the use of nonstandard English language is broken, ghetto, or slang and ultimately reflective of depravity and inadequacy. Deficit perspectives of language use during reading instruction may cause teachers to erroneously identify speakers of AAE as individuals who are in need of special education services. Special education teachers who participated in our course also engaged in tutoring within a community center that was located in a public housing community. The multicultural field placement was an important part of the course that allowed teacher candidates to reflect on consequential connections between their instruction and the sociocultural context (the community). A teacher education candidate reflected on the importance of understanding language differences when conducting a reading assessment: "The children we tutored had a different way of pronouncing certain words, but I realized it did not matter as long as he/she was reading the words correctly."

Similarly, in his seminal text *The Mis-Education of the Negro*, Carter G. Woodson (1972) addressed the ways in which teachers view nonstandard English. Woodson wrote, "In the study of language in school pupils were made to scoff at the Negro dialect as some peculiar possession of the Negro which they should despise rather than directed to study the background of this language" (p. 19). Although originally published in 1933, Woodson's words still carry a poignant and relevant message related to teachers' lack of knowledge and their misconceptions of AAE. Because teacher education programs either disregard training around speech or fail to provide in-depth understandings of the ways in which teachers' perspectives regarding multidialecticism uphold SAE myths and prejudices (Godley et al., 2015; Luke, 2004; Spring, 2016), teachers fail to recognize that language reflects linguistic antecedents, cultural identity, and sociopolitical contexts (Hilliard, 1983) and not intelligence.

Preservice teachers learning to challenge the dominant narrative regarding speech

Several bodies of research help to conceptually understand the need for greater emphasis on speech within teacher education programs. The framework below, referred to herein as the *master narrative framework*, provides insight into those bodies of research. Teachers can consider the master narrative framework as they work to expose the ways in which the history of AAE in schools, overrepresentation of AA males in schools, teachers' assumptions about speech, and speech myths around standard English converge to create problematic cycles of inequitable learning outcomes for AA males.

Master narrative framework

Language and AAE

Despite research on AAE in the 1960s and 1970s, AAE remains under-analyzed and unexplored and is believed to be largely an ahistorical language (Baldwin, 1997; Baily, 1965; Labov, 1972; Rickford & Rickford, 1976; Wolfram, 1969). *AA English* is one of a wide variety of terms used to describe the language spoken by some AAs in the United States; other terms include *Ebonics, AA Vernacular English*, and *Africanized English* (Charity, 2008; Smitherman, 1998; Perry & Delpit, 1998). Charity (2008) noted that *American English*, also referred to as *School English*, is a term used to describe English dialects that are typically used in public arenas for commerce, government, and education. Other early researchers agreed that AAE differs significantly from SAE in several aspects of its structural, phonological, lexical, syntactic, and pragmatic dimensions (Labov, 1972; Martin & Wolfram, 1998; Smitherman, 2002). Although early Western linguists characterized AAE as broken, slovenly, or poor speech that reflected the characteristic intellectual ineptness of those of African heritage (Jensen, 1969), in recent years many linguists have maintained that AAE is a systematic rule-governed language with distinctive patterns of syntax, phonology, and idiomatic expressions that are deeply rooted in the heritage of African peoples in the United States (Baugh, 2001; Rickford, 1998; Smitherman, 2002). Despite substantial scientific evidence that provides confirmation of AAE as a rule-governed language, there continues to be extensive debate around how (and to what extent) the use of AAE negatively influences reading acquisition for AA children.

An overview of the history of AAE in schools

Although school districts, teachers, and teacher preparation programs have yet to adopt the legal perspectives resulting from years of ligation surrounding AAE, we concur with Labov (1972), who proposed that "there is no reason to believe that any nonstandard vernacular is in itself an obstacle to learning. The chief problem is ignorance of language on the part of all concerned" (p. 239). One special education teacher candidate also came to the same conclusion as two historic court decisions. She stated,

> I have tried to incorporate [cultural and linguistic] experiences into my teaching. I have found that if the student and the teacher are aware that they are dealing with a different language and the different features . . . there is more clarity in instruction and learning. I feel that the emphasis on the valuing of the "inner" language of the student is crucial.

It is unfortunate that more than 40 years after the 1978 *Martin Luther King Junior Elementary School Children v. Ann Arbor School District Board* court case, language differences continue to be considered a variable that marginalizes AA youth. In this court case 15 AA students were found to be erroneously placed in special education because of their use of AAE. Based on overwhelming testimonies from linguists, U.S. District Judge Charles Joiner ruled that teachers' unconscious yet evident negative perceptions of AAE impeded students' equal access to participation in educational instructional programs (*Martin Luther King Junior Elementary School Children v. Ann Arbor School District Board*, 1979). Judge Joiner charged the Ann Arbor school board with failure to provide its teachers with adequate preparation regarding the language of AA children. Judge Joiner's decision stressed the need for teacher preparation focusing on teachers' (a) understanding of the nature of language differences in the classroom, (b) recognition of the history of language used by speakers of AAE, and (c) implementation of culturally responsive language arts pedagogies.

Another historical debate that highlighted the contentious topic of AAE in schools was the 1996–1997 Ebonics movement in Oakland, California. This movement attempted to help teachers use linguistic features of AAE to teach students SAE (Perry & Delpit, 1998). During the Ebonics debate, AA students experienced a grade point average of 1.8, and AA students represented 71% of the students placed in special education (Barnes, 2006). The Oakland School District was 53% AA during these discussions, and its school board attributed much of the failure to the language discontinuity experienced between teachers and students. The Oakland school board contended that

> numerous validated scholarly studies demonstrate that AA students as part of their culture and history an African people possess and utilize a language described in various scholarly approaches as "Ebonics" (literally Black sounds) or Pan-African Communication Behaviors or African Language Systems; and
> Whereas, these studies have also demonstrated that African Language Systems are genetically based and not a dialect of English; and
> Whereas, these studies demonstrate that such West and Niger-Congo African languages have been officially recognized and addressed in the mainstream public educational community as worthy of study, understanding, or application of its principles, laws, and structures for the benefit of AA students both in terms of positive appreciation of the language and these students' acquisition and mastery of English-language skills.

Furthermore, the school board recommended that teachers be trained in the use of AAE as an instructional method to bridge students' communication patterns between AAE and SAE. Data disaggregated by race, gender, and socioeconomic status continue to demonstrate that AA males are disproportionately harmed by teachers' insufficient knowledge of cultural differences. The persistent disproportional representation of AA male students in special education raises the question of whether we have exhausted the possibilities of appropriate preparation for general and special education teachers. The question of the influence of language when determining a language learning disability versus a language difference is not new. Yet preservice teachers too often graduate from formalized teacher preparation programs with limited exposure to the development of language, the significance of dialect and culture, and the ways in which varying dialects are falsely elevated (Hilliard, 2002) while others are viewed as defective.

Reading performance and AAE

Recent results on AA students' reading performance have revealed the urgent need to address the complex nature of underachievement through multiple avenues. Results of the National Assessment of Educational Progress (2015) indicate that the average fourth-grade reading score for AA students is 26 points lower than that of their Euro-American peers. Statistically speaking, the reading achievement gap between AA and Euro-American fourth-grade students has not closed much during the past decade. More alarming is that on average by the end of eighth grade only 16% of AA boys are at or above proficient in reading compared to 44% of their Euro-American male counterparts (National Assessment of Educational Progress, 2015). Overall, approximately 80% of AA students fail to demonstrate the ability to comprehend challenging reading texts, apply analytic skills to benefit from texts, and subsequently apply knowledge gained through reading to real-world problems.

Researchers offer numerous explanations for these disparities. Some of the more popular explanations include (a) the presence of a mismatch between the school language used by teachers and found in textbooks and the language spoken by students, which creates a stumbling block to reading acquisition (Blanchett et al., 2003; Fogel & Ehri, 2006; Godley et al., 2015); (b) the existence of teacher bias, whereby teachers characterize the speech patterns of AAs as imperfect imitations of Standard English and conclude that the students require remediation (Losen & Orfield, 2002; Miller-Jones, 1989); and (c) the presence in many schools of a school atmosphere absent of meaningful cultural representation and lacking in general appreciation for diversity (Delpit & Dowdy, 2002; Rist, 1970; Ladson-Billings, 1999). These findings, and the continued debate surrounding socially constructed variables that contribute to academic underperformance, deserve continued investigation in research on teacher education programs.

Discussions about teachers' perceptions and attitudes regarding AAE have garnered some attention within previous research. LeMoine and Hollie (2007) concluded that discussions in teacher preparation programs of how to best promote positive attitudes toward speakers for whom SAE is not their first language deserve better attention if we are to ensure equitable education for all students. Some experts assert that exposure to dialectal differences, even to a limited degree, helps to positively modify dispositions toward AAE in teacher education candidates (Bowie & Bond, 1994; Fogel & Ehri, 2006; LeMoine & Hollie, 2007). For instance, in a study conducted by Bowie and Bond (1994), preservice teachers were surveyed about their attitudes toward AAE, and three key findings emerged. The majority of preservice teacher responses were aligned with one of three categories: responses that (a) indicated a belief that AAE operates under a faculty grammar system and does not sound as good as standard English, (b) supported a general goal of standardization of English language in schools, or (c) reflected social acceptance of AAE yet rejected the use of AAE in schools. The findings also indicated that teacher candidates with even a limited amount of exposure to the topic exhibited greater positive responses regarding AAE.

Scholars have previously proposed that knowing basic linguistic and language principles may assist teachers in distinguishing between a language disability and language difference. These scholars operate from the premise that this basic knowledge may change teachers' attitude toward speakers of nonstandard English. Early examples of teacher attitudes toward ethnicity/ race and language intersectionality were provided by Goodman and Buck (1973). Goodman and Buck (1973) found that teachers with less knowledge of AAE were more likely to correct dialect-based errors during oral reading. They surmised that such interference impedes student comprehension by directing readers' attention to language accuracy and away from reading for meaning. Washington and Miller-Jones (1989) discovered that second-grade teachers' knowledge of phonological, syntactic, and stylistic components of AAE was significantly related to the way in which teachers addressed student miscues during oral reading with AA students who readily used AAE. Those teachers with more knowledge of AAE demonstrated more incidences of instructional practices found to align with best practices for reading development. These instructional practices included teacher-student interactions that fostered reading development through more student self-regulation and enhanced independent decoding strategies, which allowed for increased depth of processing. As Goodman and Buck (1973) contended, "The solution to reading problems of divergent speakers lies in changing the attitude of teachers" (p. 6).

Teachers' cultural familiarity with nonstandard English dialects might increase their self-efficacy, pedagogical persistence, and fidelity to instructional best practices when teaching students from culturally (and linguistically) diverse backgrounds (Banks, 2013; Gay, 2000; Cartledge & Kourea, 2008; Kea & Utley, 1998; Ladson-Billings, 1999). Consequently, there are pragmatic reasons to include discussions of AAE as central to the debate on overrepresentation. An understanding of diverse forms of English, teacher knowledge of the histories of culturally and linguistically diverse students, as well as the ways in which schools facilitate or hinder the academic success of diverse learners all can lead teachers to develop more affirming dispositions toward speakers of AAE.

AA boys, teacher perceptions, and language

AA boys have often been caught in the crosshairs of intersecting hegemonic narratives about race, gender, and socioeconomic status for decades. Through the years, researchers have documented how the stylistic behavioral patterns that are culturally appropriate for AA boys and their peers may be in conflict with behavior that is expected of successful students in a classroom environment (Bacon, Jackson, & Young, 2004; Harper, 2009; Johnson, 2006; Neal, McCray, Webb-Johnson, & Bridgest, 2003). For example, a verbal play that often occurs among AA boys is known as *the dozens*, or *signifying* (Hale, 1986; Wald, 2012). Playing the dozens is an interactive, competitive style of communication in which two participants exchange witty metaphors to insult other students or their family members (Wald, 2012). Teachers might misperceive the exchange as overly aggressive verbal threats or an attempt to verbally intimidate others. AA boys' cultural style of movement has also been misrepresented. AA males' walking style – often known as the *stroll* or *swagger* – is often misinterpreted by teachers as threatening and evidence of behavior that undermines academic achievement in the educational environment (Neal et al., 2003). Although AA males' behavior and language styles allow for unique demonstration of their personal identity and verbal verve, and consequently provide a sense of group identity with other AA males, these stylistic cultural behaviors often contribute to the mischaracterization of AA males as a dangerous threat (Collins, 2016). It is therefore reasonable to believe that teachers bring to the classroom societal stereotypes. These cultural deviations from mainstream, Western society become conflated into deviant notions of intellect that contribute to the misidentification of AA males as students with disabilities.

A statement from a teacher education candidate, in conjunction with the literature on teacher attitudes, highlights the unique responsibility of teacher preparation programs to provide explicit instruction to preservice teachers on the way in which speech is used to uphold hegemonies that create inequalities for AA males. This teacher candidate who completed our reading course offered the compelling observation that "the [course] readings made me think that assessment data are used almost as punishment and to point students' differences." We also note that, despite limited reading outcomes on national standardized reading assessments (National Assessment of Educational Progress, 2015), AA males possess nonstandard English language skills that contribute positively to reading performance. For example, a recent study indicated that AA preschool boys demonstrated sophisticated oral narrative skills, or storytelling skills, which positively influenced their reading abilities by sixth grade (Gardner-Neblett, Pungello, & Iruka, 2012). Yet curriculum-based interventions often fail to account for story construction, originality, and the use of a wide variety of story structures. Moreover, nationally standardized assessments (e.g., the Wechsler Intelligence Scales for Children–V, Woodcock–Johnson IV, Peabody Picture Vocabulary Test–4, Expressive Vocabulary Test–2) commonly used in the identification of students with special needs do not assess the cultural skills demonstrated by AA male students. Teachers may find that building on students' assets by fostering storytelling skills would be a beneficial and culturally responsive multitiered intervention strategy for AA boys that enhances reading skills in later grades.

Currently, of typically identifiable student groups, AA boys are at the greatest risk of being labeled with a disability (Ford, 2012; Harry & Klingner, 2014; Moore, Henfield, & Owens, 2008). More specifically, in educational settings, AA students represent approximately 17.13% of the total public school population but account for more than 26% of the children served in special education classrooms (Aud et al., 2011; Ford, 2012). AA male students represent only 9% of the total school-age population, yet they constitute a third of the students in public schools labeled with an intellectual disability. In the categories of learning disability and emotional disturbance, AA males are disproportionately represented, accounting for 12% and 21%, respectively (Aud et al., 2011). Furthermore, AA students identified as learning disabled are 3 times more likely to receive services in a separate setting; they 7 times more likely to receive services in a separate setting if they are identified as speech language impaired (Skiba, Poloni-Staudinger, Gallini, Simmons, & Feggins-Azziz, 2006). More alarming is that once labeled as having a disability, AA students are less likely than their Euro-American counterparts to be exited from special education and more likely to exhibit lower achievement gains while in special education (Aud et al., 2011). Current educational statistics provide evidence of significant educational failures for AA male students. The causes of the overrepresentation of AA male students in special education and students' reading failure are multifaceted and complex. However, current researchers continue to produce overwhelming evidence that "unconscious racial bias, stereotypes, and other race-linked factors have a significant impact on the patterns of identification, placement, and quality of services for minority children" (Losen & Orfield, 2002, p. xxii).

Teacher education and AAE language myths

The use of teacher candidate narratives throughout this article provides insight into the transformations special education teacher candidates experienced as they were exposed to the histories of AAE while learning about literacy pedagogies. The brief narratives demonstrate that teacher education candidates began to think about the dilemma that exists in appropriately identifying culturally and linguistically diverse students as students with special needs (e.g., whether a teacher can appropriately distinguish between culturally and linguistically diverse students with intrinsic language learning disabilities and those with environmental language differences). The teacher candidates in our course found it important to affirm the existence of students' plurality in their ways of thinking, talking, behaving, and learning while advancing an instructional agenda of bi-dialecticism. DeBose (2007) explained bi-dialecticism as the process used by educators when they affirm the utilitarian value of speaking Standard English even as they also "affirm the rights of speakers of all language varieties to speak them with pride and assurance" (p. 42). Knowledge and understanding of students' language backgrounds allowed teacher candidates to validate the students' cultural capital and integrate these funds of knowledge in meaningful ways into the classroom (Garcia & Ortiz, 2008; Harry & Klingner, 2014).

We must also recognize that teacher candidates may have limited understanding of the multiple historical perspectives that impact their interactions with AA children. Ladson-Billings (1999) stated, "[Teacher candidates'] historical thinking and the development of the history curriculum via textbooks makes it unlikely that prospective teachers come into teacher preparation with any sense of history and its impact on our current social, political, and economic situation" (p. 224). More teacher education courses are needed that are designed to address teacher candidates' dispositions toward AAE and move them toward more culturally responsive pedagogies. Over time, some educators may begin to examine their own instructional practices as mediated by cultural assumptions that are situated in cultural historical stereotypes. This multiple historical perspective is important in teacher candidates' understanding of how their actions contribute to what Appelbaum (2004) and Blake and Cutler (2009) characterized as institutional oppression, or discriminatory practices that are built into education. We must engender in teacher candidates a desire to reverse these trends. Because teacher education programs either disregard preparation around language or fail to provide in-depth understandings about the ways in which teachers' perspectives regarding multi-dialecticism uphold SAE myths and prejudices (Godley et al., 2015; Luke, 2004; Spring, 2016), AA male students continue to find themselves disproportionately represented in classrooms for students with language and learning disabilities. Hilliard (1983) appropriately reminded us that language reflects linguistic antecedents, cultural identity, and sociopolitical contexts and not intelligence.

Conclusions

It is not those in power, it is us, common folk like you and me. And it is not just poverty, and dialects and race that are the impetus for untoward treatment, it also includes those who are obese, mentally ill, the elderly, and other disabilities. When we use the word power it assumes someone out there, and hence we are not prompted to examine our own actions. Many of these prejudices are things we learned as children in our homes and have perpetuated as adults. Without a serious wake up call, many people never let go of these thinking patterns. It's simply too easy and quite insufficient to say it is those in power who are at fault.

(Special education teacher candidate)

Language diversity is a critical component of cultural competence. Cultural competence is essential when addressing the learning needs of historically marginalized populations, such as AA males, who may speak in nonstandard ways. Yet the topic of AAE has largely been disregarded in discussions of diversity and the achievement gap. There is increased acknowledgment among educators of the substantial need to instill in teachers an appreciation of the dynamic and intersecting components of diversity, including language. Once understood, diversity can ideally be incorporated meaningfully into conversations and solutions that seek to address institutions' bias and address inequitable learning outcomes. Teacher education programs have typically responded to this need by placing an emphasis on issues of social justice in connection with a concentration on English language learners (Lucas & Villegas, 2013); however, the translingual experiences of AA students are not typically included. Indeed, the topic of AA linguistic histories is often missing from discussions of equity and even courses focused on reading and language development for diverse learners.

The incorporation of sociolinguistic theory into discussions of overrepresentation has been somewhat underdeveloped, often because teacher educators themselves are unsure of the history of AE and AAE. Simultaneously, special education teaching pedagogies silently push to normalize students into the dominant society while ignoring the necessity of cultural agency (Patton, 1998). The relationship between AAE and the limited educational expectations afforded to AA children is not a new topic, nor is the discussion of how schools should attend to such concerns in the classroom. What this study adds to the existing body of research is an understanding of the growing trend toward intersectionality and how critical pedagogy can inform pedagogical practice in teacher education programs. This understanding has the potential to improve educational outcomes for AA male students and other culturally and linguistically diverse students.

References

Adams, M., & Bell, L. A. (2015). *Teaching diversity for social justice*. 3rd edition. New York, NY. Routledge.
Alim, H., Rickford, J., & Ball, A. F. (2016). *Raciolinguistics: How language shapes our ideas about race*. New York, NY: Oxford University Press.
Appelbaum, B. (2004). Social justice, education, moral agency, and the subject of resistance. *Educational Theory, 54*(1), 59–72.

Aud, S., Hussar, W., Kena, G., Bianco, K., Frohlich, L., Kemp, J., . . . Haynes, G. (2011). *The condition of education 2011. U.S. Department of Education, National Center for Education Statistics.* Washington, DC: U.S. Government Printing Office.

Bacon, E., Banks, J., Young, K., & Jackson, F. (2007). Perceptions of AA and European American teachers on the education of AA boys. *Multiple Voices for Ethnically Diverse Exceptional Learners, 10*(1–2), 160172.

Bacon, E., Jackson, F., & Young, K. (2004). Voices of African American boys with behavior problems: Perspectives on schooling. *Multiple Voices for Ethnically Diverse Exceptional Learners, 8*(1), 1–16.

Baily, B. L. (1965). Toward a new perspective in Negro English dialectology. *American Speech, 40*(3), 170–177.

Baldwin, J. (1997). If Black English isn't a language, then tell me, what is? *The Black Scholar, 27*(1), 5–6.

Banks, J. A. (2013). The construction and historical development of multicultural education, 1962–2012. *Theory into Practice, 52*(Sup1), 73–82.

Barnes, J. (2006). The continuing debate about 'plain language' legislation: A law reform conundrum. *Statute Law Review, 27*(2), 83–132.

Baugh, J. (2001). Coming full circle: Some circumstances pertaining to low literacy achievement among African Americans. In J. L. Harris, A. G. Kamhi, K. E. Pollock (Eds.), *Literacy in African American Communities* (pp. 277–288). Mahwah, NJ: Lawrence Erlbaum Associates, Inc.

Blake, R., & Cutler, C. (2003). AAE and variation in teachers' attitudes: A question of school philosophy? *Linguistics and Education, An International Research Journal, 14*(2), 163–194. doi:10.1016/S0898-5898(03)00034-214.

Blanchett, W. J., Klingner, J. K., & Harry, B. (2009). The intersection of race, culture, language and disability: Implications for urban education. *Urban Education, 44*(4), 389–409.

Bowie, R. L., & Bond, C. L. (1994). Influencing future teachers' attitudes toward Black English: Are we making a difference? *Journal of Teacher Education, 45*(2), 112–118.

Cartledge, G., & Kourea, L. (2008). Culturally responsive classrooms for culturally diverse students with and at risk for disabilities. *Exceptional Children, 74*(3), 351–371.

Charity, A. H. (2008). AAE: An Overview. *Perspectives on Communication Disorders and Sciences in Culturally and Linguistically Diverse Populations, 15*(2), 33–42.

Charity-Hudley, A. H., & Mallinson, C. (2010). Communicating about communication: Multidisciplinary approaches to educating educators about language variation. *Language and Linguistics Compass, 4*(4), 245–257.

Collins, K. (2016). A DisCrit perspective on The State of Florida v. George Zimmerman: Racism, ableism, and youth out of place in community and school. In D. J. Connor, B. A. Ferri, & S. A. Annamma (Eds.), *DisCrit: Disability Studies and Critical Race theory in education* (pp. 183–201). New York, NY: Teacher College Press.

Cross, J. B., DeVaney, T., & Jones, G. (2001). Pre-service teacher attitudes toward differing dialects. *Linguistics and Education, 12*(2), 211–227.

DeBose, C. E. (2007). The Ebonics phenomenon, language planning, and the hegemony of standard English. In H. S. Alim & J. Baugh (Eds.), *Talkin Black talk: language, education, and social change* (pp. 30–42). New York, NY: Teacher College Press.

Delpit, L. (2006). *Other people's children: Cultural conflict in the classroom.* New York, New York: The New Press.

Delpit, L., & Dowdy, J. K. (2002). *The skink that we speak: Thoughts on language and culture in the classroom.* New York, NY: The New Press.

Dyson, A., & Smitherman, G. (2009). The right (write) start: African American language and the discourse of sounding right. *The Teachers College Record, 111*(4), 973–998.

Fogel, H., & Ehri, L. C. (2006). Teaching AAE forms to standard American English-Speaking teachers: Effects on acquisition, attitudes, and responses to student use. *Journal of Teacher Education, 57*(5), 464–480.

Ford, D. (2012). Culturally different students in special education: Looking backwards to move forward. *Exceptional Children, 78*(4), 391–405.

Freire, P. (1970). *Pedagogy of the oppressed.* New York, Seabury Press.

Garcia, S., & Ortiz, A. (2008). A framework for culturally and linguistically responsive design of response-to-intervention models. *Multiple Voices for Ethnically Diverse Exceptional Learners, 11*(1), 24–41.

Gardner-Neblett, N., Pungello, E. P., & Iruka, I. U. (2012). Oral narrative skills: Implications for reading development of AA children. *Child Development Perspectives, 6*(3), 218–224.

Gay, G. (2000). *Culturally responsive teaching: Theory, practice, and research.* New York: Teachers College Press.

Giroux, H. (1997). *Pedagogy and the politics of hope theory, culture, and schooling: A Critical Reader.* New York, NY. Routledge.

Godley, A., Reaser, J., & Moore, K. (2015). Pre-service English language arts teachers' development of critical language awareness for teaching. *Linguistics and Education, 32*(A), 1–14.

Goodman, K., & Buck, C. (1973). Dialect barriers to reading comprehension revisited. *Reading Teacher, 27,* 6–12.www.jstor.org/stable/20193381

Hale, J. (1986).Black children: Their roots, culture, and learning styles.Baltimore: Johns Hopkins University Press.

Harper, S. R. (2009). Niggers no more: A critical race counternarrative on Black male student achievement at predominantly White colleges and universities. *International Journal of Qualitative Studies in Education, 22*(6), 607–712.

Harry, B., & Klingner, J. (2014). Why are so many minority students in special education?: Understanding race and disability in schools. New York, NY: Teacher College Press.

Hill, J. (2008). *The everyday language of white racism.* Oxford, England: Wiley-Blackwell.

Hilliard, A. (1983). Psychological factors associated with language in the education of the African American child. *Journal of Negro Education, 52*(1), 24–34.

Hilliard, A. G. (2002). Language, culture, and the assessment of AA children. In L. Delpit and J. K. Dowdy (Eds.), *The Skin that We Speak: Thoughts on language and culture in the classroom* (pp. 89–105). New York, NY: The New York Press.

Jensen, A. R. (1969). How much can we boost IQ and scholastic achievement? *Harvard Educational Review, 39*(1), 1–123.

Johnson, P. D. (2006). Counseling African-American men: A contextualized humanistic perspective. *Counseling and Values, 50*(3), 187–196.

Kea, C. D., & Utley, C. A. (1998). To teach me is to know me. *The Journal of Special Education, 32*(1), 44–47.

Koehler, M. J., Mishra, P., Kereluik, K., Shin, T. S., & Graham, C. G. (2013). *The technological pedagogical content knowledge framework. Handbook of research on Educational Communications and Technology* (pp. 101–111). New York, NY: Springer.

Labov, W. (1969). *A study of non-standard English. U.S. Department of Health, Education, & Welfare.* District of Columbia: Center for Applied Linguistics.

Labov, W. (1972). *Language in the inner city: Studies in the Black vernacular.* Philadelphia, PA: University of Pennsylvania Press.

Ladson-Billings, G. (1999). Preparing teachers for diversity: Historical perspectives, current trends and the future directions. In L. Darling-Hammond, & G. Sikes (Eds.), *Teaching as the learning profession: Handbook of policy and practice* (pp. 211–247). San Francisco, CA: Jossey Bass.

Lareau, A. (1987). Social class difference in family-school relationships: The importance of cultural capital. *Sociology of Education, 60*(2), 73–85.

LeMoine, N., & Hollie, S. (2007). Developing academic English for standard English learners. In H. S. Alim & J. Baugh (Eds.), *Talkin Black talk: language, education, and social change* (pp. 43–55). New York, NY: Teacher College Press.

Losen, D. J., & Orfield, G. (2002). Racial inequity in special education. In D. J. Losen & G. Orfield (Eds.), *Racial inequality in special education* (pp. xv–xxxviii). Cambridge, MA: Harvard Education Press.

Lucas, T., & Villegas, A. M. (2013). Preparing linguistically responsive teachers: Laying the foundation in preservice teacher education. *Theory into Practice, 52*(2), 98–109.

Luke, A. (2004). On the material consequences of literacy. *Language and Education, 18*(4), 331–335.

Martin Luther King Junior Elementary School Children v. Ann Arbor School District Board. (1979). Civil Action No. 7-71861, 473 F. Supp.1371.

Martin, S., & Wolfram, W. (1998). The sentence in African American vernacular English. In S. S. Mufwene, J. R. Rickford, G. Bailey, & J. Baugh (Eds.), *African-American English: Structure, history, and use.* New York, NY: Routledge Press.

Miller-Jones, D. (1989). Culture and testing. *American Psychologist, 44*(2), 360–366.

Moore, J. L., Henfield, M. S., & Owens, D. (2008). African American males in special education: Their attitudes and perceptions toward high school counselors and school counseling services. *American Behavioral Scientist, 51*(7), 907–927.

National Assessment of Educational Progress. (2015). *The Nation's Report Card. Institute of education sciences.* Washington, D.C.: U.S. Department of Education.

Neal, L., McCray, A. D., Webb-Johnson, G., & Bridgest, S. T. (2003). The effects of African American movement styles on teachers' perceptions and reactions. *The Journal of Special Education, 37*(1), 49–57.

Paige, K., & Hardy, G. (2018). Science as a human endeavor, critical pedagogy and practitioner inquiry: Three early career cases. *International Journal of Science and Mathematics Education*, 1–221. doi: 10.1007/s10763-018-9887-x

Patton, J. M. (1998). The disproportionate representation of African Americans in special education: Looking behind the curtain for understanding and solutions. *The Journal of Special Education*, *32*(1), 25–31.

Perry, T., & Delpit, L., (1998). *The real Ebonics debate: Power, language, and the education of African-American children.* Boston, MA: Beacon Press.

Rickford, J. (1999). *African American vernacular English: Features, evolution, educational implications.* Hoboken, NJ: Wiley-Blackwell.

Rickford, J. R. (1998). The creole origins of African-American English: Evidence from copula absence. In S.S. Mufwene, J.R. Rickford, G. Bailey, & J. Baugh (Eds.), *AAE: Structure, history, and use* (pp. 411–424). New York, NY: Routledge.

Rickford, J. R., & Rickford, A. E. (1976). Cut-eye and suck-teeth: African words and gestures in new world guise. *Journal of American Folklore*, *89*(353), 294–309.

Rist, R. (1970). Student social class and teacher expectations: The self-fulfilling prophecy in ghetto education. *Harvard Educational Review*, *40*(3), 411–451.

Sanders-Smith, S. C., & Gaumer, N. (2016). Working together for support math pedagogy: It all adds up for students. In S. Bernoteit, J. C. Ernst, & N. I. Latham (Eds.), *Voices from the Field: Collaborative Innovations in Early Childhood Educator Preparation* (pp. 163–178). Illinois Education Research Council & Illinois Board of Higher education: Edwardsville, IL.

Shulman, L. S. (1986). Those who understand: Knowledge growth in teaching. *Educational Researcher*, *15*(2), 4–14.

Shulman, L. S., & Shulman, J. H. (2004). How and what teachers learn: A shifting perspective. *Journal of Curriculum Studies*, *36*(2), 257–271.

Skiba, R. J., Poloni-Staudinger, L., Gallini, S., Simmons, A. B., & Feggins-Azziz, R. (2006). Disparate access: The disproportionality of African American students with disabilities across education environments. *Exceptional Children*, *72*(4), 411–424.

Smitherman, G. (1977). *Talkin and testifying: The language of Black America.* Detroit, MI: Wayne State University.

Smitherman, G. (1998). *Talkin and testifyin: The language of Black America.* Wayne, MI: Wayne State University Press.

Smitherman, G. (2002). Toward a national public policy on language. In L. Delpit & J. Dowdy (Eds.), *The skin that we speak: Thoughts on language and culture in the Classroom* (pp. 163–178). New York: New York Press.

Spring, J. (2016). *Deculturalization and the struggle for equality: A brief history of the education of dominated cultures in the United States.* New York, NY: Routledge.

Wald, E. (2012). *Talking 'bout your mama: The dozens, snaps and the deep roots of rap.* Oxford, London: Oxford University Press.

Washington, V., & Miller-Jones, D. (1989). Teacher interactions with strong and weak speakers of nonstandard English during reading instruction. *Contemporary Educational Psychology*, *14*(3), 280–312.

Wilkinson, I. A., Reznitskaya, A., Bourdage, K., Oyler, J., Glina, M., Drewry, R., & . . . Elson, K. (2017). Toward a more dialogic pedagogy: Changing teachers' beliefs and practices through a professional develop in language arts classrooms. *Language and Education, 31*(1), 65–82.

Wolfram, W. A. (1969). *A sociolinguistic description of Detroit Negro speech.* Washington DC: Center for Applied Linguistics.

Wolfram, W. (2011). The *African American English* canon in sociolinguistic. In M. Adams and A. Curzan (eds.), *Contours of English and English Language Studies.* Ann Arbor: University of Michigan Press, pp. 34–52.

Woodson, C. G. (1933). *The mis-education of the Negro.* New York: AMS Press.

4 Teaching writing to young African American male students using evidence-based practices

Steve Graham, Karen R. Harris,
and Keith Beard

There are long-standing concerns about boys and writing in the United States. As a group, boys do not write as well as girls (see Berninger & Fuller, 1992; Walberg & Ethington, 1991). This was evident in the last National Assessment of Educational Progress, on which Grade 8 girls scored 19 points higher than Grade 8 boys on the writing assessment and Grade 12 girls scored 14 points higher than Grade 12 boys (National Center for Education Statistics, 2012). Males who are African American may be particularly at risk for experiencing challenges learning to write, as the National Assessment of Educational Progress further found that Grade 8 students who were African American scored 22 points lower than Grade 8 White students. This gap increased to 29 points by Grade 12.

The trend for boys as well as children who are African American to score lower on writing measures does not mean that students who are male, African American, or both will experience writing difficulties. We do not draw attention to these statistics because there is a causal link among gender, race, and writing. Race, particularly through its link to poverty in the United for boys, provide information about a child's risk for developing writing difficulties (Peterson, 2006). It is critical that young African American males from economically impoverished backgrounds receive sound writing instruction to ensure that they get off to a solid start in writing. Of course, this is important for all children, regardless of race, gender, or economic condition, but it is especially important for children who do not have the same affordances as many other students.

This article examines whether evidence-based instructional practices for teaching fundamental writing skills and processes enhance the writing performance of young African American males experiencing difficulty learning to write. To determine this, we reexamined data from five previous writing intervention studies we conducted with elementary students at risk for writing difficulties. Almost all of the students in these studies lived in neighborhoods in the Washington, DC, area that were predominantly African American and poor. Our reanalysis focused just on children in each study who were African American male students.

Fundamental writing processes and skills

Writing is an extremely complex skill whose mastery has vexed many learners, young and old. At the most basic level, a writer decides what to say and how to say it, translating each idea into an acceptable sentence, transcribing each sentence into legible text with correctly spelled words, monitoring and evaluating this production process to ensure that communicative intentions and audience needs are met, and making changes to ideas and text based on these evaluations. This further requires drawing on specialized knowledge of the purpose, structure, and forms of the type of text to be produced in a particular writing community as well as marshaling the cognitive resources, effort, and persistence to start, maintain, and finish the writing task (Graham, 2018). Fundamental to the success of this enterprise are processes involving goal setting, planning, monitoring, evaluating, and revising as well as skills for sentence construction, spelling, and handwriting (when text is handwritten).

Planning

The fundamental writing process of planning is an essential ingredient in skilled writing, as skilled writers spend a considerable amount of time setting goals, generating ideas, and organizing ideas into a writing plan (Kellogg, 1987). An advanced written plan may be particularly helpful for young writers, as it provides an external repository where ideas can be stored and manipulated without the risk of forgetting them. Planning in advance further reduces the need to plan while writing, freeing up cognitive resources that can be applied to other aspects of writing, such as handwriting, spelling, and sentence construction (Kellogg, 1986).

Revising

Revising is also a fundamental process of skilled writing, as skilled writers devote up to 20% of their time revising (Hayes & Flower, 1980; Kellogg, 1987). They use revising to make adjustments in their plans as well as changes in their text during and after its initial production. The basic goal of such efforts is to improve the text and ensure that one's intentions are realized. Efforts to increase the substantive revisions made by young writers may be especially useful, as children typically make few revisions, limiting most of their revisions to superficial changes involving error correction and changes focused on individual words or phrases (Fitzgerald, 1987).

Self-regulation procedures

Skilled writers apply a variety of self-regulatory processes to help them manage the process of writing, the writing environment, and their behaviors when writing (Zimmerman & Risemberg, 1997). These procedures include goal setting, self-monitoring, self-evaluating, self-instructions, and self-reinforcing. They are used to manage and orchestrate writers' intentions, actions, and the writing environment when composing. In contrast, young writers apply an approach to writing that converts it into an act of simply telling what one knows (Scardamalia & Bereiter, 1986). Text is generated when an idea comes to mind, with each preceding idea serving as the stimulus for the next idea. This approach functions as an automated and forward-moving content generation system, minimizing the use of self-regulation procedures (McCutchen, 2000). As a result, an important instructional goal for young writers is to help them adopt an approach to writing that places greater emphasis on conscious regulation of the writing enterprise.

Sentence construction

Skilled writers have a facility for transforming ideas into the words and syntactic structures (i.e., sentences) that convey their intended meanings. The sentences they produce range from simple to complex; use grammar, punctuation, and capitalization appropriately; and are purposefully varied to meet their intentions (Kaufer, Hayes, & Flowers, 1986). Young writers, in contrast, are less efficient at constructing sentences. Their sentence skills are limited to relatively simple constructions, and they have not mastered many of the intricacies of usage and grammar (Saddler & Graham, 2005). Young children's advancement as writers is dependent on mastering more complex sentences as well as learning how to construct the sentences mastered more fluently.

Handwriting and spelling

Until transcription skills such as handwriting and spelling become efficient and relatively automatic, they exact a toll on writing (Kellogg, 1986, 1987). Having to devote conscious attention to handwriting and spelling can interfere with other writing processes (Berninger, 1999). For instance, when a child has to switch attention during writing to a mechanical demand, such as figuring out how to spell a word, he or she can forget ideas held in working memory. Illegibilities and misspellings also make it more difficult to read text, and readers may form negative judgments about a text when such problems are evident (Graham, Harris, & Hebert, 2011). Explicit instruction designed to enhance handwriting and spelling is beneficial, as young writers' spelling and handwriting improve, as do other aspects of their writing (Graham, Kiuhara, McKeown, & Harris, 2012).

Teaching writing to young African American males experiencing difficulties learning to write

Although planning, revising, self-regulation, sentence construction, handwriting, and spelling do not represent all that children need to learn to become better writers, there is scientific evidence that teaching each of these skills positively impacts students' writing (Graham et al., 2012). Although this claim applies to elementary students broadly, it is not clear whether it applies specifically to young African American males who are experiencing difficulties learning to write. In fact, the scientific literature provides little evidence on writing instruction for these students.

In most of the available investigations that have included young African American males as part of the research sample, including studies that have focused on children who are weaker writers, data on the writing performance of these children are not presented separately (Ball, 2006). For instance, Nelson (2010) investigated the effectiveness of a writer's workshop approach for African American as well as White third-grade students, some of whom had special needs and some of whom did not. Although the intervention improved all students' performance over time, including that of African American students with special needs, data were not analyzed by gender and race.

In a study with older middle school students, Yeh and Staurt (1998) explicitly taught strategies for planning and creating argumentative text. This instruction had a positive impact on the writing of African American, Asian, Hispanic, and White students, but again the data for this study were not presented or analyzed by race or gender. Similarly, Davis, Clarke, and Rhodes (1994) provided students in culturally diverse classrooms greater opportunity to write extended text, which resulted in better writing in terms of content and conventions. The researchers did not examine, however, whether instructional gains were related to gender or race (see also Kliewer et al., 2011).

Even when studies focus specifically on African American children, findings for male students are not commonly disaggregated. Fogel and Ehri (2000), for example, reported that guided grammar instruction increased the accuracy with which African American students used Standard English in their writing, but they did not determine whether gender was related to student gains. Note that Geisler, Hessler, Gardner, and Lovelace (2009) did report data separately for male and female African American students, but their study involved just five children. They found that the self-regulation procedure of self-monitoring had a positive impact on the writing output of both male and female students.

One commonality among all of the studies described above is that each of them involved an evidence-based writing practice. A writer's workshop, strategy instruction, facilitation of the use of self-regulatory procedures, and explicit instruction of skills were each identified as effective instructional practices in a meta-analysis of true and quasi-experiments by Graham et al. (2012), whereas explicit skill instruction similar to Fogel and Ehri (2000) was shown to be effective in a meta-analysis of single-subject design studies by Rogers and Graham (2008). These instructional studies also demonstrated that teaching some of the fundamental writing processes and skills described previously had a positive impact on the writing of culturally diverse students. With the exception of Geisler et al. (2009), however, these studies did not isolate the effects of such instruction for young African American males who were experiencing difficulty learning to write. To address this gap in the literature, we reanalyzed data from studies we conducted with mostly young African American elementary students who were experiencing difficulty learning to write.

Reanalysis of data from the center to accelerate student learning

From 1999 to 2005, the first two authors were part of a center designed to test writing, reading, and math interventions for students with special needs or at risk for learning problems (Graham & Harris, 2005). As part of this effort, the first two authors conducted a series of true experiments that tested the effectiveness of various writing interventions with primary grade students experiencing difficulty learning to write (i.e., the students scored at the 25th percentile or below on a writing test and teachers confirmed that the students had writing difficulties). The writing assessment used to screen students was the Test of Written Language-3 (Hammill & Larsen, 1996), which measures story writing skills. In all studies, the thematic structure of students' stories was assessed with this measure. In other studies, more discrete skills like sentence construction or spelling were also assessed depending on the focus of instruction.

The studies conducted by the first two authors all took place in the Washington, DC, area in neighborhoods that were mostly poor economically and were overwhelmingly African American. These studies examined the effectiveness of strategy instruction for planning (Graham, Harris, & Mason, 2005), using self-regulation to enhance revising (Graham & Harris, 2006), combining sentences to improve sentence construction skills (Saddler & Graham, 2005), and teaching handwriting (Graham, Harris, & Fink, 2000) and spelling (Graham, Harris, & Fink-Chorzempa, 2002).

None of these studies disaggregated data by race or gender or analyzed whether these variables moderated the impact of the writing treatments. We rectify that situation here (at least in part) by reporting effect sizes (ESs) for writing performance for African American males in each study. We computed ESs by subtracting the mean performance of African American males in the control group from the mean performance of African American males in the treatment group and dividing by the pooled standard deviation for both groups. This was done after first correcting for any pretest differences that existed between treatment and control students. We did not conduct statistical significance tests, however, as the sample size for each study was now significantly reduced, which would have increased the likelihood of committing a Type I error if such tests had been applied. We did correct ESs for small sample size bias (Hedges, 1982). An ES of 0.80 is considered to be a large effect, 0.50 a moderate effect, and 0.20 a small effect.

It is important to note that the writing interventions tested in the five studies referenced above and reanalyzed here met some of the characteristics of culturally responsive teaching (Ladson-Billings, 1994). High expectations were communicated, active teaching methods were applied, instruction mainly involved small groups, and interactive dialogue was encouraged. Within the context of these studies, instruction was designed to foster an "I can do" attitude among all students, and it was expected that all students could master the skills and strategies taught. Teachers demonstrated with help from students how to apply targeted writing skills and strategies, and students worked together collaboratively to apply these procedures. Teacher and students actively discussed the procedures they were learning and how to apply them.

Teaching advanced planning and self-regulation

In Graham et al. (2005), the self-regulated strategy development (SRSD) model (Harris, Graham, Mason, & Friedlander, 2008) was used to teach students strategies for planning and drafting stories and opinion text. This included teaching students a general planning strategy represented by the mnemonic POW: *Pick* my ideas, *Organize* my notes, and *Write* and say more.

Students were also taught genre-specific strategies for story as well as opinion writing to help facilitate the second POW step of organizing their information. The genre-specific strategy for story writing was represented by the mnemonic WWW, What =2, How-2, which prompted students to generate possible ideas for their story by considering the following questions in advance of writing: *Who* is the main character? *When* does the story take place? *Where* does the story take place? *What* does the main character do or want to do; what do other characters do? *What* happens then? *What* happens with other characters? *How* does the story end? *How-* does the main character feel; how do other characters feel? The genre-specific strategy for opinion writing was represented by the mnemonic TREE, which prompted students to generate advanced planning notes: *Tell* what you believe (State your topic sentence), give three or more *Reasons* (Why do I believe this?), *Examine* each reason (Will my reader buy it?), *End* it (Wrap it up right).

Students first learned to use POW and TREE to write opinion essays, followed by learning how to apply POW and the WWW strategy for story writing. In both instances, they were taught how to use self-regulation procedures involving goal setting, self-monitoring, self-instructions, and self-reinforcement. Collectively these self-regulation procedures were designed to help students manage the planning strategies they were learning to use, the writing process, and their behaviors when writing. All instruction involved small groups of students. We illustrate the six stages of SRSD instruction below with story writing.

Stage 1: Develop and activate background knowledge

During this stage, the teacher and students discussed the purposes and use of POW, the WWW strategy, and the self-regulation procedures. The teacher and students further read and discussed model stories, including examples of good and poor stories. This discussion also allowed the teacher to make sure students knew each of the story elements included in the WWW planning strategy. The students then discussed how positive self-statements could help improve their writing as opposed to negative self-statements. The teacher encouraged students to see writing as a fun and rewarding activity.

Stage 2: Discuss it

This stage of instruction emphasized what good writers do when planning, composing, and revising. The teacher discussed with students how POW and the WWW strategy could help them write both in and out of the classroom. The importance of student effort in learning the strategies was also emphasized, and students made a commitment to learn the planning strategies and their applications. Finally, the teacher explained that students would set goals for including basic elements in their story and graph the number of parts in each story they completed during instruction. The graph helped students visualize their progress.

Stage 3: Model it

The teacher modeled out loud how to use POW and WWW. Students participated in this modeling by helping the teacher generate ideas for the story. The teacher also provided examples of how to set personal goals for writing, self-monitor performance using the graph introduced earlier, and self-reinforce their accomplishments. Following modeling, the teacher and students discussed the things that the teacher had said to herself and why and developed one or more self-statements they would use to help them manage as they wrote.

Stage 4: Memorize it

Throughout the previous stages, students made an effort to commit to memory the POW and WWW strategies. Memorization was finalized in this stage by having students practice with one another the steps and purposes of POW and WWW.

Stage 5: Support it

In this stage, students were increasingly encouraged to take greater responsibility for using the writing strategies and accompanying self-regulation procedures. Initially they applied the strategies and self-regulation procedures with a peer, using support material such as the graphic organizer for POW and WWW to help them carry out the writing process. They then moved to using the strategies, self-regulation procedures, and support materials independently, with the goal of eliminating all support material. The teacher conferenced with students, and students shared their compositions and their progress graphs. During conferences, the teacher emphasized how effort and strategy use led to better writing in students' stories. If students did not meet their goals for a story, the teacher provided guidance on how the paper could be revised to meet the goals.

Stage 6: Independent performance

Instruction was completed when students were able to use the strategies taught to independently write (without teacher support) a story that included all of the basic parts. The teacher and students discussed how to transfer the POW, WWW, and self-regulation procedures to other literacy tasks and were encouraged to do so.

Peer support for transfer

Students were randomly assigned to a no-treatment control or one of two SRSD conditions. These were the SRSD condition described above and one that included SRSD plus peer support for transfer. In this latter SRSD condition, pairs of students met once a week to identify and discuss where one or more of the procedures they were learning could be applied. They set a goal to use one aspect of what they were learning in a new situation, discussing roadblocks and how to overcome them. When they met again, the students shared whether they met their goal, difficulties encountered, how the procedures were helpful.

The students in the Graham et al. (2005) study were in third grade, and 33 of them were African American males (nine control students, 11 SRSD students, and 13 SRSD plus peer support for transfer students). The quality of students' stories and opinion essays in the two SRSD conditions increased dramatically in comparison to the performance of the control students. The ESs for SRSD versus controls were 0.80 for stories and 1.28 for opinion essays, whereas the ESs for SRSD plus peer support for transfer versus controls were 1.24 for stories and 0.98 for opinion essays. Thus, explicitly teaching fundamental writing processes of planning and self-regulation using an evidence-based practice (i.e., SRSD; see Graham et al., 2012) enhanced the writing of young African American male students experiencing difficulties learning to write.

Graham et al.'s (2005) study was the first time that POW, TREE, and the WWW strategy were taught together. The effectiveness of one or more of these strategies was tested in multiple investigations before and after the study presented here. This included studies in which middle school students used TREE as a quick write method to facilitate learning (e.g., Mason, Kubina, & Taft, 2011), elementary students used a modified version of the WWW strategy to write better stories (Glaser & Burnstein, 2017), and students with attention-deficit/hyperactivity disorder improved their persuasive writing with TREE (Lienemann & Reid, 2008), to provide a few examples. SRSD studies in which these strategies have been taught have consistently improved students' writing performance (see Graham et al., 2012).

Revising and self-regulation

Graham and Harris (2006) worked individually with fourth-grade students experiencing difficulties learning to write to change their revising behavior so that they made better revisions and made more revisions that involved meaning changes. All students in this study participated in four instructional sessions. They first wrote a story, and then half of them (randomly determined) were asked to revise their story to make it better. In contrast to the control students (four African American males), the children in the experimental condition (six African American males) were provided four possible revision goals to choose from: (a) set it in a different time, (b) add a new character, (c) change the location, and (d) change when it occurred.

The goal setting revising treatment had a positive impact on students' revising behavior compared to the control condition, resulting in an ES of 0.97 for quality of revisions and an ES of 1.70 for number of meaning-changing revisions. Thus, the evidence-based practice of goal setting (see Graham et al., 2012) improved the revising behavior (a fundamental writing process) of young African American male students experiencing difficulty learning to write.

Sentence construction

Saddler and Graham (2005) tested the effectiveness of sentence combining, an evidence-based practice (see Graham et al., 2012). More and less skilled fourth-grade writers were paired and taught how to construct more complex sentences. An identical arrangement was applied for control students, except they were taught grammar skills. Seven African American males who were weaker writers were in the sentence-combining group; four were in the control condition (students had been randomly assigned to the two conditions).

The sentence-combining treatment was organized into five units. The first unit focused on combining small sentences into a compound sentence using the conjunctions *and*, but, and because. The second unit involved the addition of an adjective or adverb from one sentence to the other (e.g., "They walk to the park" and "They walk slowly" combined to "They walk slowly to the park"). The third and fourth units focused on creating complex sentences by incorporating an adverbial or adjectival clause from one sentence into the other (e.g., "The car stopped" and "The light turned red" combined to "The car stopped when the light turned red"). The final unit extended the skills taught in Units 2–4 by teaching students to make multiple embeddings with adjectives, adverbs, adverbial clauses, and adjectival clauses (e.g., "John opened his eyes," "John was in a hospital," "John called for a nurse," and "John wanted some water" combined to "John, who was in a hospital, called for a nurse because he wanted some water").

In each unit, sentence-combining instruction involved the teacher first explaining and modeling how to combine two smaller sentences as a larger one to achieve the desired goal (e.g., forming a compound sentence). The paired students then practiced combining sentences orally and in writing, with the teacher providing feedback as needed. This guided practice was followed by independent practice, with each member of the pair discussing and evaluating his or her solutions. An open-ended exercise was then introduced in which students were asked to combine multiple sentences. This exercise contained 10 to 20 sentences that told a story. Students were instructed to combine the sentences by adding connecting words, taking out unneeded words, moving words around, and changing word endings. Last, students applied the sentence-combining skills they had learned as they wrote and revised their own compositions.

As students were learning to combine sentences in each unit, cues to facilitate the process were initially provided but faded as the student pairs practiced. These cues provided examples of specific words that had to be included in order to combine the sentences correctly.

The evidence-based practice of sentence combining had a positive impact on the fundamental writing skill of sentence construction for the young African American males experiencing difficulty learning to write who participated in this study. An ES of 0.31 was obtained on a sentence construction measure, favoring the sentence-combining group. In addition, compositions written after instruction by these students were qualitatively better than the compositions written by the grammar-instructed controls (ES = 0.14).

Spelling

Graham et al. (2002) provided spelling instruction to second-grade children experiencing difficulties learning to write. Half of the children in their study were randomly assigned to spelling (eight African American males) or math (17 African American males) instruction. Students in both instructional conditions were taught in small groups. Spelling instruction consisted of 48 lessons divided into eight units. Each 2-week unit of six lessons contrasted two or more spelling patterns (e.g., short vowel vs. long vowel). During the first lesson of each unit, the teacher directed a word-sorting activity designed to help students discover and state the rule underlying the target spelling patterns. The teacher first showed students a master word card for each spelling pattern (e.g., /mad/ for the short vowel pattern and /made/ for a long vowel pattern). Each word was pronounced with the teacher emphasizing the vowel sound. Using several more cards with words that fit one of the target patterns, the teacher modeled while thinking out loud why each new word would be placed with one of the master words (e.g., /had/ with /mad/). When doing so, the teacher used both sound cues (e.g., emphasizing the vowel) and letter cues (e.g., pointing out the consonant-vowel-consonant pattern). Students were encouraged to form hypotheses about the rules underlying each pattern and test them as the teacher and students sorted additional words. This activity ended with the teacher and students stating a rule for each spelling pattern. Students were encouraged to locate and share as many words that fit the spelling patterns as they could over the course of the unit.

Starting in the second lesson and continuing forward, students were given the choice to use two different approaches to learning eight words that fit the targeted patterns (all words occurred frequently in students' writing, and students had misspelled each on a pretest). The first procedure, called *graph busters*, involved the following steps: (a) say the word and study the letters, (b) close your eyes and say the letters, (c) study the letters again, (d) write the word three times without looking at it, and (e) check the spellings and correct any misspellings. The students marked their progress in studying words with this method by graphing how many times they practiced words in a lesson. The second procedure involved studying the words while playing one or more games that required students to spell a word correctly in order to move forward.

During the second lesson and continuing forward, students engaged in two additional activities. In a peer-directed activity, students identified which letter(s) corresponded to a sound represented at the beginning, middle, or end of objects depicted in pictures. Students also worked together to build words that corresponded to the spelling patterns they were learning during that unit. They were provided with a rime (/ad/) on a card and 18 other cards that contained different consonants, consonant blends, and diagraphs (i.e., onsets). They were directed to put the rime and onsets together to identify as many real words as possible within the allotted time.

When we examined just the performance of the African American male students in this study, we found that explicit teaching of a text transcription skill, an evidence-based practice (see Graham et al., 2012), improved a fundamental writing skill, spelling, and this instruction enhanced students' sentence construction skills and reading performance too. On two spelling tests, the ESs for the spelling treatment (vs. math instruction) were 0.64 and 0.47. Spelling instruction also resulted in ESs of 0.96 for sentence writing, 1.04 for reading word recognition, and 0.50 for reading word attack.

Handwriting

In a study by Graham et al. (2000), first-grade students experiencing difficulties learning to write were individually taught three lowercase manuscript letters per week (except in the last week, which included just two letters). Letters taught during a week shared common formational characteristics (e.g., /a/ and /c/), and letters that are easily confused with each other were not grouped together (e.g., /b/ and /d/). Letters that occurred more frequently in children's writing were taught first (e.g., /o/, /e/, /a/), as they were easier to form letters (e.g., /l/, /i/, /t/).

Each letter set was taught in three lessons, and each lesson had a similar format. First, students engaged in tasks designed to teach them to identify each letter of the alphabet by name, match the names with the appropriate letters, and identify where each letter in the alphabet was placed. Second, the three letters in each set were taught and practiced. The teacher modeled and described how to form each letter. Students then imitated the teacher's models of how to form the letters, which was followed by a discussion of the similarities and differences in the letters. Next the students practiced writing each letter (in the second and third lessons this was done in the context of words), with students circling their best formed letters. Third, students copied a sentence containing multiple instances of the letters from the current and previous weeks for a period of 3 min. They copied this text as neatly but as quickly as possible. In each succeeding lesson, they were asked to set a goal to increase the number of letters written in the 3-min period. Fourth, students were taught how to take one taught letter and write it in an unusual way (e.g., such as fat or long) or as part of a picture (e.g., turning an i into a bird).

Half of the students in Graham et al.'s (2000) study were randomly assigned to the handwriting treatment and half were assigned to phonological awareness instruction. The seven African American males in the handwriting condition made greater gains in handwriting fluency, writing quality, and sentence construction than the 10 African American boys in the phonological awareness control condition. The ESs for these three measures, respectively, were 1.01, 0.54, and 0.75. Explicit teaching of a text transcription skill, an evidence-based practice (see Graham et al., 2012), improved two fundamental writing skills, handwriting and sentence construction, as well as the quality of text produced by young African American males experiencing difficulties learning to write.

Summary

In this article, we reexamined data from five true experiments we conducted in the Washington, DC, area (mostly in poor neighborhoods). The students in these studies were overwhelmingly African American elementary students experiencing difficulty learning to write. Our new analysis focused only on the African American children who were males and experienced writing difficulties. We wanted to determine whether teaching these students fundamental writing skills and processes (i.e., planning, revising, self-regulation, sentence construction, spelling, and handwriting) using evidence-based practices (i.e., SRSD, goal setting, sentence combining, and explicit instruction; see Graham et al., 2012) would enhance their writing. This proved to be the case. Teaching planning and self-regulation procedures had a large and positive impact on students' writing (ESs were 0.80 or greater for quality of story and opinion writing), as did setting goals to make specific structural changes when revising a story (ESs were 0.97 or greater for measures of revising behavior) and handwriting instruction (ES = 1.01 for handwriting fluency). Moderate and positive effects were obtained for sentence combining (ES = 0.31 for sentence construction skills) and spelling instruction (ESs ranged from 0.47 to 0.64 for spelling measures). Just as important, sentence combining as well as handwriting and spelling instruction enhanced other writing skills (e.g., sentence construction), whereas spelling instruction resulted in improved reading skills.

Care must be taken in interpreting the findings from our reanalysis because of the relatively small number of African American male students in each study. Nonetheless, our results clearly support the contention that the writing performance of young African American male students experiencing difficulty learning to write can be enhanced when they are provided with evidence-based practices designed to improve fundamental writing skills and processes. Additional research is needed to replicate these findings and to anchor the instruction provided in these studies more firmly within other culturally relevant teaching practices (Ladson-Billings, 1994). This includes writing about topics that are more relevant to students culturally and personally as well as making home and classroom connections for writing a prominent part of the instructional process.

References

Ball, A. (2006). Teaching children in culturally diverse classrooms. In C. MacArthur, S. Graham, & J. Fitzgerals (Eds.), *Handbook of writing Research* (pp. 293–310). NY: Guilford.

Berninger, V. (1999). Coordinating transcription and text generation in working memory during composing: Automatic and constructive processes. *Learning Disability Quarterly*, 22(2), 99–112.

Berninger, V., & Fuller, F. (1992). Gender differences in orthographic, verbal, and compositional fluency: Implications for assessing writing disabilities in primary grade children. *Journal of School Psychology*, 30(4), 363–382.

Davis, A., Clarke, M., & Rhodes, L. (1994). Extended text and writing proficiency of students in urban elementary schools. *Journal of Educational Psychology*, 86, 556–566.

Fitzgerald, J. (1987). Research on revision in writing. *Review of Educational Research*, 57(4), 481–506.

Fogel, H., & Ehri, L. (2000). Teaching elementary students who speak Black English vernacular to write in standard English: Effects of dialect transformation practice. *Contemporary Educational Psychology*, 25, 212–235.

Geisler, J., Hessler, T., Gardner, R., & Lovelace, T. (2009). Differential writing interventions for high-achieving urban African American elementary students. *Journal of Advanced Academics*, *20*, 214–247.

Glaser, C., & Burnstein, J. (2017). Improving fourth-grade students' composition skills: Effects of strategy instruction and self-regulation procedures. *Journal of Educational Psychology*, *99*, 297–310.

Graham, S. (2018). A writer(s) within community model of writing. In C. Bazerman, V. Berninger, D. Brandt, S. Graham, J. Langer, S. Murphy, P. Matsuda, D. Rowe, & M. Schleppegrell (Eds.), *The lifespan development of writing.* (pp. 271–325) Urbana, IL: National Council of English.

Graham, S., & Harris, K. R. (2005). Improving the writing performance of young struggling writers: Theoretical and programmatic research from the center to accelerate student learning. *The Journal of Special Education*, *39*(1), 19–33.

Graham, S., & Harris, K. R. (2006). The effects of goal setting in revising on the revising behavior and story writing of fourth grade struggling writers. Presentation at Pacific Coast Research Conference, CA.

Graham, S., Harris, K. R., & Fink, B. (2000). Is handwriting causally related to learning to write? Treatment of handwriting problems in beginning writers. *Journal of Educational Psychology*, *92*(4), 620–633.

Graham, S., Harris, K. R., & Fink-Chorzempa, B. (2002). Contributions of spelling instruction to the spelling, writing, and reading of poor spellers. *Journal of Educational Psychology*, *94*(4), 669–686.

Graham, S., Harris, K. R., & Hebert, M. (2011). It is more than just the message: Analysis of presentation effects in scoring writing. *Focus on Exceptional Children*, *44*(4), 1–12.

Graham, S., Harris, K. R., & Mason, L. (2005). Improving the writing performance, knowledge, and motivation of struggling young writers: The effects of self-regulated strategy development. *Contemporary Educational Psychology*, *30*(2), 207–241.

Graham, S., Kiuhara, S., McKeown, D., & Harris, K. R. (2012). A meta-analysis of writing instruction for students in the elementary grades. *Journal of Educational Psychology*, *104*, 879–896.

Hammill, D., & Larsen, S. (1996). *Test of written language - 3*. Austin, TX: Pro-Ed.

Harris, K. R., Graham, S., Mason, L., & Friedlander, B. (2008). *Powerful writing strategies for all students*. Baltimore, MD: Brookes.

Hayes, J., & Flower, L. (1980). Identifying the organization of writing processes. In L. Gregg & E. Steinberg (Eds.), *Cognitive processes in writing* (pp. 3–30). Hillsdale, NJ: Erlbaum.

Hedges, L. V. (1982). Estimation of effect size from a series of independent experiments. *Psychological Bulletin*, *92*(2), 490–499.

Kaufer, D., Hayes, J., & Flowers, L. (1986). Composing written sentences. *Research in the Teaching of English*, *20*, 121–140.

Kellogg, R. (1986). Designing idea processors for document composition. *Behavior Research, Methods, Instruments, and Computers*, *18*(2), 118–128.

Kellogg, R. (1987). Effects of topic knowledge on the allocation of processing time and cognitive effort to writing processes. *Memory & Cognition*, *15*(3), 256–266.

Kliewer, W., Lepore, S., Farrell, A., Allison, K., Meyer, A., Sullivan, T., & Greene, A. (2011). A school-based expressive writing intervention for at-risk urban adolescents' aggressive behavior and emotional lability. *Journal of Clinical Child and Adolescent Psychology, 40*(5), 693–705.

Ladson-Billings, G. (1994). *The dreamkeepers: Successful teachers of African American children.* San Francisco: Jossey-Bass.

Lienemann, T. O., & Reid, R. (2008). Using self-regulated strategy development to improve expository writing with students with attention-deficit/hyperactivity disorder. *Exceptional Children, 74*(4), 471–486.

Mason, L., Kubina, R., & Taft, R. (2011). Developing quick writing skills of middle school students with disabilities. *The Journal of Special Education, 44*(4), 205–220.

McCutchen, D. (2000). Knowledge, processing, and working memory in writing and writing development. *Educational Psychologists, 35*(1), 13–24.

National Center for Education Statistics. (2012). *The nation's report card: Writing 2011.* Washington, D.C.: Institute of Educational Sciences, U.S. Department of Education.

Nelson, N. (2010). Changes in story probes written across third grade by African American and European American students in a writing lab approach. *Topics in Language Disorders, 30*(3), 223–252.

Peterson, S. (2006). Influence of gender in writing development. In C. MacArthur, S. Graham, & J. Fitzgerald (Eds.), *Handbook of writing research.* NY: Guilford.

Rogers, L., & Graham, S. (2008). A meta-analysis of single subject design writing intervention research. *Journal of Educational Psychology, 100,* 879906.

Saddler, B., & Graham, S. (2005). The effects of peer-assisted sentence combining instruction on the writing performance of more and less skilled young writers. *Journal of Educational Psychology, 97*(1), 43–54.

Scardamalia, M., & Bereiter, C. (1986). Written composition. In M. Wittrock (Ed.), *Handbook of research on teaching* (3rd ed., pp. 778–803). New York: MacMillan.

Walberg, H., & Ethington, C. (1991). Correlates of writing performance and interest: A U.S. National assessment study. *Journal of Educational Research, 84*(4), 198–203.

Yeh, S., & Staurt, S. (1998). Empowering education: Teaching argumentative writing to cultural minority middle school students. *Research in the Teaching of English, 33,* 49–83.

Zimmerman, B. J., & Risemberg, R. (1997). Becoming a self-regulated writer: A social cognitive perspective. *Contemporary Educational Psychology, 22*(1), 73–101.

Index

Note: Numbers in bold indicate tables and numbers in italics indicate figures on the corresponding page.